D1251331

ETYMOLOGICAL DICTIONARIES

ETYMOLOGICAL DICTIONARIES

A Tentative Typology

Yakov Malkiel

The University of Chicago Press · Chicago and London

YAKOV MALKIEL is professor of linguistics and Romance philology
at the University of California, Berkeley. He has been editor-in-chief of
Romance Philology since 1947. His many publications include
Studies in the Reconstruction of Hispano-Latin Word Families (1954),
Directions for Historical Linguistics (1968),
and *Essays on Linguistic Themes* (1968).

THE UNIVERSITY OF CHICAGO PRESS, CHICAGO 60637
THE UNIVERSITY OF CHICAGO PRESS, LTD., LONDON

© *1976 by the University of Chicago*
All rights reserved. Published 1976
Printed in the United States of America

Library of Congress Cataloging in Publication Data

Malkiel, Yakov, 1914-
  Etymological dictionaries.

  Bibliography: p.
  Includes indexes.
  1. Language and languages—Etymology. 2. Encyclopedias and
dictionaries—History and criticism.
  I. Title.
P321.M33   412   75-11866
ISBN 0-226-50292-9

412
M25

CONTENTS

PREFACE

Approximately one hundred years ago, William D. Whitney, in one of the classics of nineteenth-century linguistics, *The Life and Growth of Language,* declared emphatically that etymology, i.e., the study of word origins, was the cornerstone of any progressive, truly scientific inquiry into language. Few practitioners and even fewer theorists of general linguistics today would subscribe to such a flattering assessment of the role of etymology, a discipline whose fall from high estate, accelerated over the last thirty or forty years, has been quite dramatic. True, in certain domains of specialized research, to this day philologically flavored, the preeminence of old-style etymology remains undisputed. But since it is general linguistics which has emerged as tone-setting in our own time, it is clear that a rehabilitation of etymology, through vigorous rejuvenation of its presuppositions and techniques, cannot be achieved by assiduous, painstaking accumulation of data alone. It requires the periodic cleansing and, if necessary, the bold replacement of antiquated tools, so as to enable etymologists to engage in a dialogue with other scholars on a high level of generality.

Etymology, then, has lost a battle but not the war, provided some of its devotees are willing to take the risk of seeing its challenges, assets, and liabilities in a new perspective. Experience teaches us that knowledge advances often in cycles — better still, in spirals. To lift an endangered discipline out of its current doldrums, one must attempt to pull it up and push it forward at the same time, so as to avoid monotonous repetition. Microglottology, which has etymology at its core, is, I believe, potentially as vital and as promising as ever, and its further decay, which might have very bad consequences for a whole bundle of scholarly pursuits in the general realm of spatio-temporal linguistics, ought to be averted at almost any cost. But a generous measure of experimentation and the eagerness to take risks are the price one must be prepared to pay for such abandonment of rote.

The present typological survey of etymological dictionaries marks just one step in this direction. Typological analysis is no substitute for time-honored historical accounts or detailed, plodding descriptions (exhaustive "inventories," the delight of bibliographers). But sometimes it affords striking perspectives, which are apt to give prominence to issues that may otherwise have remained deeply buried or, at least, hidden from view. The organization of an entry in an etymological dictionary is, for instance, an issue briefly hinted at, in pragmatic terms, in numerous prefaces and introductions to such dictionaries, but seldom if ever isolated as a complex problem worthy of searching discussion.

The author of one etymological dictionary, concerned with, say, language X, obviously feels obliged to consult at every second step similar lexicographic compilations, for languages Y, Z, etc., on account of the need to explain many loanwords; but after satisfying his hunger with little "bites," he seldom pauses to study in leisurely, systematic fashion the architectural design of those other dictionaries he falls back on in casual consultation. Thus, ironically enough, drops of knowledge, bearing on minute facts, are rapidly diffused, but the relevant vessels serving to contain knowledge elude systematic comparison. Here typology seems to provide the best remedy yet discovered.

Undeniably − as I happen to know from personal experience − there exist more dizzying problems of both theory and spadework in etymology than that presented by a mere survey of dictionaries, however sophisticated its blueprint. In undertaking this particular task, which forms part of a major strategic plan, I have been telling myself that advanced lexical research, with very rare exceptions, is based in large part on dictionaries, primarily on etymological dictionaries; and that, granted the usual margin of mediocrity, some of these have been truly original masterpieces. Thus studying specimens of their fabric in depth involved an austere but by no means pedestrian operation, reminiscent of the musicologist's investigation into the wealth of available instruments as a preliminary to, or a concomitant of, such reputedly more exciting disciplines as harmony and composition. There was one additional, even more compelling reason for choosing the survey form: Given the extraordinary complexity of conditions surrounding the growth of words, today's etymologists − assuming they are courageous but not foolhardy − will tend to shrink back from the discussion of problems involving more than, say, two language families. While an occasional twentieth-century virtuoso, like Sapir or Trubetzkoj, may have indulged the privilege of juggling, with impressive

PREFACE

results, over one hundred diverse languages on the level of phonology or of grammar, the extension of such performances to the lexical domain has become forbiddingly hazardous. When I first experimented, in the mid and late 'fifties, with the typological classification of (a) etymological solutions, (b) historical grammars, and (c) (variously slanted) dictionaries, I limited myself almost exclusively to Romance material, and I do not regret this self-confinement. Conversely, the organization of etymological dictionaries, as distinct from the check on the accuracy of etymological equations, allows one to transcend with relative impunity the bounds of one's own narrower domain. I found it entertaining to cast a quick glance at the state of affairs in Icelandic, Coptic, and Nepalese and hope that, in so doing, I have avoided the worst pitfalls.

There remains for me the pleasant duty of acknowledging the help or encouragement of several friends. Peter F. Dembowski showed himself once more a master strategist in establishing the much-needed personal contact with the publisher. Henry Kahane, who at my own request was invited to assess the manuscript as an expert, turned out to be not only an erudite and sharp-eyed, but also a sensitive and understanding reader. The bulk of the typescript was prepared, with great care, cheerfulness, and empathy, by Leanna J. Gaskins, who, as a young philologist in her own right, volunteered in the process several bits of valuable advice. Mary-Louise Hansen, being an inspired stylist, greatly improved the wording of several chapters. Judith E. Pinson lent her help in deftly — and promptly — typing numerous inserts and additions. Though most of the bibliographic information was gathered in Berkeley, I availed myself of an extended research travel to Europe, in the spring of 1974, to fill certain gaps; I am, consequently, grateful to the authorities of my own university for granting me a sabbatical leave of absence plus a travel allowance, and to my European hosts, for making my pilgrimage worthwhile.

Berkeley, 7 June 1974

1

PRELIMINARIES AND A PANORAMIC
VIEW OF THE PROBLEM

There is no need, at this late date, to offer any justification for the typological approach to the study of languages. Conversely, a few scattered experiments, in a not too distant past, with the application of typological analysis to certain genres of scholarly inquiry have not yet produced any major impact,[1] so that the wisdom of engaging in such work remains in abeyance. In advocating it, one may argue that just as it is feasible and recommendable to write histories of the major and even the minor genres (e.g., "Where, when, and how did the formal study of lexical doublets start?") or to compile specialized bibliographies (e.g., one of historical or of contrastive grammars), so it seems worthwhile to explore the range of possibilities in an atlas, a dialect monograph, a grammatical sketch, etc., by decomposing such ventures into their constituents and by examining how successive schools of thought or individual authors have gone about interpreting each such constituent and in what ways these constituents can be put together so as to produce a viable whole.

Since we have not yet gone beyond the experimental stage in such probings, it seems advisable to heed the voice of practicality in matters of sheer size of material. In an earlier study, all manner of lexicographic compilations (descriptive, historical, normative, even jocose) were surveyed, but strictly in reference to a single major European language. This time, I expect to be more narrowly selective as regards the character of the lexicographic compilations examined (only etymological dictionaries of varying slants and structures are to be included); this confinement to a single category of reference work is to be offset by inclusion of a wide variety of languages, beyond the bounds of Indo-European, even though completeness of coverage will not be one of my aims.

The criteria of selection are to be loose; since the purpose of the survey is not utilitarian or pedagogical, there seems to be little point in limiting oneself to the latest or the reportedly best dictionaries of this

1

sort. Easily the most rewarding assortment will include some writings deemed at present antiquated, but once esteemed as authoritative; in this way shifts in tastes and in criteria of excellence are apt to stand out quite sharply in retrospect. Concern with the full range of structural diversity must override all other canons in classifications so slanted. The first major step in the preparation of a typological survey is the discovery of certain distinctive features. One such feature is TIME DEPTH. Assuming an etymological dictionary of modern English is satisfied with leading the reader, wherever possible, to the time level of Chaucerian usage: such a guide will differ radically from another dictionary whose compiler insists on tracing characteristic words all the way either to Old English, or to Proto-Germanic, or even beyond.

A second such feature is the DIRECTION, or PROJECTION, OF ETYMOLOGICAL ANALYSIS. Analysis can be prospective, as when the starting point chosen is a recorded (or reconstructed) "parent language" viewed in relation to its "daughter languages" — say, Latin vis-à-vis the full spectrum of Romance languages; or, less ambitiously, in relation to a single member of that family. Alternatively, analysis is retrospective, when the observer selects, as his point of departure, a later stage, e.g., modern Portuguese, then traces each relevant word to its ancestral source, be it Latin, or Greek, or Arabic, or Provençal, or Old French, or "substratal."

A third feature qualifying for classificatory purposes is the RANGE of the dictionary. One can agree, with respect to source languages, that only the principal ancestor be focused upon or taken into account (e.g., Latin vis-à-vis Rumanian — to the exclusion of Slavic, Hungarian, Middle Greek, Turkish, Albanian, and "proto-Balkanic," all of which are also represented in the Rumanian vocabulary). With respect to the target language(s), one envisages an even greater diversity and fluctuation of possible approaches: a single language in its distilled literary form, with or without archaisms; a single literary tongue with full attention to its principal dialectal variations (or, at least ideally, to all of them); the most prominent members of a language family (G. Körting's "romanische Haupt-sprachen"); all known members of such a family; a superstock. There further emerge several defensible hierarchies: in a comparative etymo-logical dictionary all members, one gathers, are — almost by definition — treated on a par, but there also, paradoxically, exists the so-called comparative dictionary of a single language, i.e., one in which the

2

language chosen as the prime target is treated exhaustively and the others only in ancillary or auxiliary fashion, by way of "background." One may regard as the fourth distinctive trait the TOTAL ORGANIZATION OF THE CORPUS, the lexicographer's GRAND STRATEGY. The material may be offered consecutively, without major subdivisions, with one entry following upon the other and all entries being similarly organized (cf. M. Vasmer's dictionary of Russian) — except for minor qualifications, as when in Meyer-Lübke's comparative Romance dictionary all reconstructed bases are set off, in Schleicherian fashion, through a prefixed superscript asterisk. For a while, it was fashionable to number the entries successively (among Romance scholars, G. Körting did so for the first time in 1891, and Meyer-Lübke unwisely perpetuated the habit as late as 1930-35); the disadvantage of the procedure consists in that, with each revision of a given standard work, intercalary numbers have to be inserted — undeniably an eyesore and a nuisance. Even worse, the deletion of certain entries belatedly recognized as untenable produces embarrassing gaps in the sequence of numbers.

Over against this familiar pattern, certain famous dictionaries, especially those written in the nineteenth century, show deep cleavages; thus, August Fick, in the 1870-71 edition of his tone-setting comparative Indo-European dictionary — after Bopp the first monumental venture of its kind — divided his material along spatio-temporal lines, examining first the lexicon of the IE "Ursprache," turning his attention next to the words of the "Common Aryan Phase," and concentrating afterward on smaller units or speech communities ("Spracheinheiten") recognized at that juncture: European, Graeco-Italic, Slavo-Germanic, etc. Even before that date, Diez (1853) separated pan-Romanic words, which he listed in the order of their Italian representatives, from those peculiar to certain individual branches of Romance. One readily conceives yet other policies of gross divisions, even if they have never been implemented. Thus, after G. Gröber, in his trail-blazing "Vulgärlateinische Substrate," had segregated from the bulk of Romance words those traceable to reconstructed bases, nothing would have hindered him from launching the project of a Latin-Romance dictionary in two parts, the watershed being the philological status of each base: recorded in ancient texts versus internally reconstructed. Another possibility that comes to mind — implied in Meyer-Lübke's technique though never exploited by that scholar — would have been to

3

treat separately the Romance trajectories of Latin bases transmitted by word of mouth and those bequeathed through learned channels. In harmony with the mainstream of German cultural tradition one could set off the Germanic patrimony (*Erbwörter*) from early borrowings, thoroughly assimilated (*Lehnwörter*), and from superficially adjusted foreignisms (*Fremdwörter*). Finally, the decision whether selectivity or exhaustiveness should be aimed at also falls under grand strategy.

Still within the confines of grand strategy one can usefully discuss such broad-gauged matters as the policy presiding over the listing of variants, compounds, and affixal derivatives; the controversial issue of a dictionary's ideal size, and certain ramifications of this problem, e.g., the risk of overextension, and the techniques available for compression; the special handling of languages displaying two, or more, neatly distinguishable strains, or, alternatively, of two languages closely associated, indeed, paired off, in a given cultural context, as have been for centuries Classical Hebrew and Biblical Aramaic, and consequently inventoried, as a rule, in the same dictionary – often one etymologically slanted.

The fifth distinctive feature, and the one demanding particularly scrupulous, microscopic inspection, is the FAVORED STRUCTURING OF THE INDIVIDUAL ENTRY. On this point, which discloses the analyst's TACTICAL PREFERENCES, no two dictionaries seem to be alike. One cluster of problems surrounds the crucial decision: Should the lexical family in all its morphological ramifications, or the individual word, with careful attention to all its semantic nuances and to its evolutionary metamorphoses, function as the ideal unit ("entry")? Even for this single organizational issue there has been proposed a whole scale of solutions. The grouping of words in major families – Ernout and Meillet's Latin dictionary (1932) comes to mind at once – suggests an attempt at systematization which seems to involve a concession to structuralism and to smack of modernity. Actually, the procedure is not at all modernist: S. de Covarrubias, for one pioneer, resorted to it over three and a half centuries ago. The reverse procedure, namely the furnishing of a separate etymological base for each member of a family, is scientifically unhelpful; nevertheless, it carries with it an advantage in casual consultation, eliminating as it does the need for numerous cross-references and catering as it also does to the commodiousness of the lay reader. Between the extremes of loose fragmentation and of bold bracketing, or subsumption, under a common denominator one recognizes numerous transitions, as when

4

only the closest derivatives or the most transparent cognates are grouped together. Another compromise was toyed with by Meyer-Lübke, who listed as separate entries, in conventional fashion, all words encountered or reconstructed at the level of the source languages (Latin, Frankish, Gothic, etc.), but added Romance (i.e., innovative) suffixal derivatives and compounds to the inventory of the vernacular reflexes of each ancestral base listed.

The order in which the vernacular representatives are paraded before the reader also varies significantly. It may be in the alphabetical sequence of the names of the languages, with Albanian preceding Zend; in their geographic sequence, with Rumanian leading via Rhaeto-Romance to Galician-Portuguese; or in terms of their relative archaicity, with Sardinian and northern French representing the two poles. (The last-mentioned possibility, however defensible, seems not yet to have been tried out.) Finally, data and analysis may be closely enmeshed, or outwardly separated, by differences of font and paragraphing, as in Wartburg's *FEW*, though in reality the arrangement of the raw data of itself reflects a generous quota of previous analysis.

One may, somewhat arbitrarily, label as BREADTH — the sixth distinctive feature here invoked — the inclusion of all manner of auxiliary, ancillary, and background information, either within the nucleus of the given dictionary, as part of the statements and discussions supplied under the entries, or segregated from that kernel and offered as "forematter" or as a supplement. Again, the possibilities are practically unlimited, even if one disregards such routine aids as lists of abbreviations, formal bibliographies, and indexes (whose presence or absence often spells the difference between ready availability and virtual inaccessibility of vital information). The more typical manifestations of breadth inside the entries are glimpses of historico-archaeological situations, with heightened attention to material civilization; slivers of geographico-dialectological conditions; bits of philological documentation (hints of writers and periods, quotations of characteristic passages, references to loci); nuggets of grammatical analysis (*lato sensu*), i.e., references to moot points of graphemics, phonology, morphology, syntax, semantics, poetics, and style; and, above all, bibliographic clues to earlier etymological discussions. These can be crisp and matter-of-fact, despite their copiousness (Walde and Hofmann, Wartburg); or equipped with incisive, if restrained, critical remarks (Gamillscheg, Meyer-Lübke); or discursive and overtly polemic (Corominas). Note that under certain circumstances — e.g., where an overgrowth of discussions threatens to produce the stifling impression of a "jungle" — the complete elimination of this apparatus may have a wholesome effect, as is true of Ernout and Meillet's classic and, on a more modest scale, of Migliorini and Duro's *Prontuario* and Dauzat's *DÉLF*. Sometimes, the reduced "popular" edition of a monumental venture is marked by omission of such details; cf. Corominas' *Breve diccionario* vis-à-vis his unabridged *DCE*, and O. Bloch and W. von Wartburg's concentrated *DÉLF* vis-à-vis the latter author's overflowing *FEW*.

Discussions extraneous to the dictionary proper are apt to be of two kinds. Either they involve questions of broad methodology, as is particularly true of prefaces written by prestigious leaders of the profession operating on a higher intellectual level than the authors (one thinks of the Indo-Europeanist Meillet's preface to O. Bloch's dictionary of French, or of the pan-Romanist Meyer-Lübke's preface to A. Nascentes' dictionary of Portuguese); or they are attempts at stock-taking or self-appraisal (or, more modestly, self-characterization) by the authors, an attitude not infrequently combined with a critique of the gropings of their immediate predecessors; finally, they may aim at enlightening the reader on the best use he can possibly make of the book. It is also conceivable that an introduction to an etymological dictionary provides, by way of a handy frame, a panoramic view of the period of incubation or of the hiatus between source language and target language involved. A separate systematic digest — never yet assayed — of all such prefaces and introductions is overdue and would be highly desirable as a contribution to the history of linguistics. As regards appendixes, all kinds of afterthoughts and excursuses come to mind — starting with the simplest case of straight addenda made at page proof (Körting, Meyer-Lübke, Corominas), even though certain scholars (e.g., T. Burrow and M. B. Emeneau as the joint authors of a Dravidian etymological dictionary) have preferred to issue, after an appropriate lapse of time, a formal supplement volume and still later, by way of aftermath, one additional article-sized collection of gleanings.

Far and away the most elusive of all these possibilities for elaboration are the snippets of information on historical grammar with which every etymological dictionary, almost by definition, must be replete. Especially in contexts where relatively simple original developments appear to have become embroiled through secondary and tertiary shifts (as is true, for instance, of the Old Spanish sibilants) every single word biography counts, and the etymological dictionary, for all its avowed "pointillisme," will be consulted as assiduously as the corresponding handbook of phonology.

It is perhaps legitimate to appeal in this context to the label "scope" — as distinct (indeed, arbitrarily differentiated) from "breadth" and "range," whose use we have already preempted — to introduce a seventh discrete classificatory criterion. Let SCOPE, then, stand for the PARTICULAR SELECTION OR ASSORTMENT OF MATERIAL favored by the etymologically-minded lexicographer. While the overview of the given community's total lexicon ("thesaurus") remains an ideal goal, more difficult to achieve than a "concordance," all sorts of practical considerations conspire to bias or twist the material selected for analysis. The words chosen may be those most frequently used (though commonness of occurrence is hardly a relevant factor in etymology), or those most anciently recorded, or those once used but later doomed to extinction, or else, conversely, those traceable to older periods but still tolerated or, at least, marginally understood as archaisms. Where downright dead languages, such as Hittite or Tocharian or Ugaritic, are involved, such programmatic limitations would be pointless; but where hard-boiled commercial publishers sponsor dictionaries of "modern" languages which boast a glorious past (English, French, or Spanish, say), conflicts are apt to arise between the author's, the publisher's, and the reader's views as to where (if at all) obsolete items should come up for dissection. Further limitations, for the most part less controversial, arise where a dictionary project aims only at a single level, or register, of speech (colloquial, broadly literary, advisedly academic, etc.); where a particular genetic "strain" or "streak" (e.g., Arabisms in Spanish) or a combination of such streaks (e.g., Oriental words in German, or Amerindian words in European tongues) is to receive exclusive attention; or where a particular text, or author, or a literary school tied together by a homogeneous style (lexicon included) emerges as a frame of reference, as is true of etymological vocabularies devoted — in the past — to a Chrétien de Troyes or a Juan Ruiz, and as could some day be true, in a new crop of cross-linguistic dictionaries, of those exploring the proclivities of Mannerism, Baroque, Romanticism, or Symbolism.

The eighth and — at this stage of investigation — last dimension is the CHARACTER of the etymological dictionary. The two basic distinctions concern the AUTHOR'S PURPOSE and the LEVEL OF TONE. In regard to authorial intention, one takes it for granted that only scientifically-objective writings should be taken into account.

7

However, passionate etymological concern has entered also into tendentious writings – those departing from the straight path on the basis either of political prejudice, or of an intellectual whim, even "craze," or of both (Celto- and substrato-mania, Maurophilia, Germanophobia, or what not). Sadly enough, PARTISANSHIP has even generated etymological alertness.

Finally, there exists in certain cultures, at given moments, a "gray zone" of etymology pursued for the sake of its ENTERTAINMENT value, with all sorts of piquancies flowing from this definition, or, at least, practice. What complicates immensely the imbroglio is the fact that slivers of information extracted from unorthodox varieties of etymology can be profitably used in serious research. Even where the purpose of the book is unassailably serious, the tone may vary – in an unbroken gradient – from (a) overtly erudite via (b) scholarly but generally accessible to (c) designedly diluted for popular consumption. It is safer not to include under "character" the dimension of "coverage" (actually exhaustive, aiming at reasonable completeness but falling short of exhaustiveness, frankly and consistently selective), which has already been dealt with in a different niche.

It is difficult to imagine an etymological dictionary that cannot be succinctly described or "coded" through the joint application of these eight autonomous criteria.

These dimensions or parameters by no means exhaust the classificatory possibilities; one is at liberty to toy with extensions of the system here proposed – in several directions, for that matter. One additional parameter could very well be the INTENDED DURABILITY of an etymological dictionary, since quickly executed stopgap operations and long-term projects involving a lifetime of unremitting labor clearly constitute two extremes of a continuum. The avowedly temporary solution is exemplified by W. Spiegelberg's *Koptisches Handwörterbuch* (1921) – which is etymological, even though the title is noncommittal. The author used a six-month period of enforced leisure, plus thirty years of earlier experience, to "ram through" a selective emergency dictionary (involving Coptic-Egyptian correspondences) which, he anticipated, would soon be replaced by a far more solidly carpentered structure. Over against such a designedly temporary building one could place W. von Wartburg's *FEW*, spanning sixty years of one single-minded man's unrelieved dedication. Obviously most authors are coyly reticent about their own expectations as to the survival of their books. Another defensible dimension could be the degree of CENTRALITY OF THE ETYMOLOGICAL COMMITMENT: Thus, the *Thesaurus Linguae Latinae* is, essentially, a kind of concordance invaluable on account of the passages quoted, but its crisp etymological comments (some of them initialed by Meyer-Lübke, hence decidedly authoritative) represent a mere sideline, while other dictionaries, e.g., that of English prepared by Onions and his team, concentrate on their etymological commitment. Yet another possibility, in certain respects particularly stimulating but also very hazardous, would be to use as a yardstick each author's STYLE OF ETYMOLOGICAL ANALYSIS and the underlying LINGUISTIC CREED. It has for decades been customary to discriminate between phono-etymological and semo-etymological proclivities (A. Thomas vs. H. Schuchardt), and of late one attempt has been made to set off a pattern of morpho-etymological preferences as well. In all three instances, I decided against complicating my machinery at this moment, while leaving open the possibility of further exploring these hazily defined dimensions.

This essay is predicated on the assumption that the etymological dictionary (vocabulary, glossary) is a reasonably well-defined genre of scholarly inquiry and a neatly delimited source of information. The assumption is borne out by a number of circumstances, including the trivial but hardly negligible fact that there has existed on the book market, for well over a century, a category of reference books known as "etymological dictionaries." Even this fact, extraneous to linguistic analysis though it is, invites elaboration, inasmuch as both commercial publishing houses and academic publishers on the European continent (as well as university presses in the English-speaking countries) have produced books of widely varying merit, circulation, and appeal titled "etymological dictionaries." One is free to distinguish between such dictionaries on the popular level, written to satisfy the curious layman, and others, on the strictly scholarly level, prepared for the exclusive convenience of the specialist. It is also possible to set off an intermediate plateau of shorter etymological dictionaries – shorn of their erudite apparatus and adapted to the use of the average – or the "typical" – educated reader – but composed by such authoritative scholars as to command the attention of experts, especially where "capsulized" verdicts on controversial issues are involved.

Whatever the level aimed at and attained, it is essential to remember that, counter to expectation, the use of the tag "etymological" in the title of a reference work carries with it no guarantee of etymological relevance. One readily visualizes two major deviations from the promise implicit in such a tag. On the one hand, a first-rate dictionary serving a variety of different worthwhile purposes may include among the services it offers its readers also drops of finely distilled etymological information. In the late nineteenth century, Émile Littré's and Darmesteter-Hatzfeld's superbly documented and edited dictionaries of French furnished the best available etymological hypothesis as just one of several clues. Good bilingual dictionaries – cf. H. Tiktin's for Rumanian and German – may include slivers of etymological information; so may modern editions of older bilingual glossaries (cf. the three Latin-Spanish ones – dating from ca. 1400 – annotated by A. Castro; also C. Tagliavini's edition of the Latin-Rumanian-Hungarian *Lexicon Marsilianum* and L. Gáldi's edition of S. Klein's *Dictionarium Valachico-Latinum*). Even a primarily syntactic dictionary, such as R. J. Cuervo's unfinished venture, may, incidentally, contain priceless nuggets of etymological knowledge.

The reverse situation can also be documented with concrete cases. Because the label "etymological" carried with it a certain exaggerated prestige in the past, especially around 1850, not a few antiquarians, local historians, and amateur dialectologists compiled all sorts of regional vocabularies, chiefly in France (e.g., Charles Beauquier, 1881; Jules Corblet, 1851; Gabriel Lévrier, 1867), but also in other countries, which they qualified, perhaps upon the advice or at the urging of their aggressive publishers, as "etymological," although such etymologizing as the authors had engaged in was – at least from our vantage – unoriginal, dilettantish, plagiaristic, or worse.

Ironically, the relative loss of the social prestige of historicism in our own century and the decline of etymological preoccupation among most – though by no means all – front-line linguists have led to a wholesome cleansing in the use of "etymological," a trend which has already benefited dictionaries as well as other classes of research. Today, etymology has, for better or worse, become a minority concern but, by the same token, an indisputably serious one, and once this disinfection has been completed, the discipline will stand poised for reconquest of lost ground.

At the outset, we preferred not to distinguish too sharply between dictionaries, vocabularies, and glossaries, provided they were etymologically slanted, on the tacit understanding that in loose usage these three terms are pressed into service almost interchangeably, while in more careful terminology their referents differ chiefly as to size, density of network, and wealth of verbal illustration, but hardly in essence. Certain Italian scholars (e.g., Bruno Migliorini) have cultivated, as a separate variety, the etymological *prontuario,* i.e., 'compendium' or 'guide,' which generally denotes and connotes a less energetic commitment or stakes out a more modest claim to originality. Common to all these subclasses is the inclusion of a cross-section of the lexicon of the chosen language or languages; a monographic study of phytonyms, or kinship terms, or color adjectives, or prepositions, or verbs of motion may constitute a very attractive lexicological task, but is divorced from lexicography, which ideally operates on the total of a lexical corpus, or, by way of concession to realities of life, on balanced reductions therefrom.

The term "etymological," strictly speaking, requires no further qualification, since "etymology" has definitively lost its previous ambiguity ("study of word origins" ~ "morphology"). J. Corominas' fairly recent insistence on self-portrayal as "crítico-etimológico," in an attempt, one gathers, to forestall any possible confusion of his brainchild with compilations executed in a popular or amateurish vein, smacks of anachronism, reminding the sophisticated reader of certain treatises characteristic of the eighteenth century. Only Z. Gombocz's significantly earlier Hungarian dictionary shows the same idiosyncrasy.

Of all rival categories the "etymological" dictionary comes closest to its "historical" counterpart. Yet, despite a certain undeniable overlap, the two varieties do not coincide, since etymology places the highest premium on the prehistory of words − pieced together through imaginative if judicious reconstructions − whereas the dictionary committed to a historical approach enables its user to assemble the philologically documented segments, or rather fragments, of the given words' itineraries. In practice, the success of reconstruction obviously hinges in large measure on the analyst's thorough familiarity with the most archaic pieces of the available corpus of evidence. As a result, historical and etymological dictionaries are best used side by side, and the professional etymologist, in his quest for improvements, will again and again scan the material garnered and sifted by the language historian (and vice versa). Despite this generous amount of interlocking, the emphases in these two genres of diachronic research remain intrinsically different.

It is even more difficult to trace a cogent borderline between etymological dictionaries and all sorts of historically tilted onomastic

11

reference works; e.g., alphabetically arranged lists of place names, river names, first names, family names, etc., in which each entry begins with an etymological vignette. In actual laboratory work, the frontier between the two domains becomes fuzzy and may even altogether vanish: important common nouns may have been preserved solely in proper names, especially in toponyms, oronyms, or hydronyms, while even irreducibly "pure" anthroponyms may, upon occasion, shed oblique light on otherwise concealed features of sound development. Despite this constant overlap, certain arguments, more convincing on the practical than on the theoretical side, can be adduced in favor of continued separation of the genuine lexicon from the stock of proper names (which, to begin with, are, in point of grammatical behavior, invariably nouns – even though verbs, etc., have been derived from some of them).

In referring to dictionaries we have so far taken for granted their alphabetical arrangement – with minor allowances for special local conditions (see chapter 5). There exists on the market, of course, a minority group of ideological or semantic dictionaries – with very old antecedents; but these, as a rule, either carry no etymological information whatever, or, if they do, happen to be quite undistinguished on the side of etymological pronouncements – with the noteworthy exception of Isidorus' *Origines.* In this respect they differ from inquiries into smaller slices of the lexicon presided over by some semantic "common denominator," such as plant and animal names (including H. Palander-Suolahti's investigation [1899] of the Old High German names of mammals), kinship and anatomical terms (one is reminded of the pioneering studies, at the turn of the century, by the Romanists E. Tappolet [1895] and A. Zauner [1902] – preceded by the Indo-Europeanist B. Delbrück [1885]), or calendar units (Fr. Miklosich's analysis of the Slavic names of the months goes back to 1868). Fine-meshed studies so biased very often – though by no means obligatorily – contain a strong component of original etymological research, but hardly qualify for inclusion in the category here selected any more than do loose strings of etymological notes (some of them conceivably very elaborate) that have, for convenience's sake, been arrayed in alphabetical sequence just before the monograph went to press.

Though we are here concerned with subclasses or salient features of etymological dictionaries rather than with the personalities or biographies or bibliographies of etymologists and lexicographers, a few remarks on the typical position such dictionary projects occupy in the careers and commitments of linguistic scientists seem to be permissible. The monographic, microscopic investigation of a single etymological problem frequently represents a pilot study preceding, or a companion piece flanking, a full-blown dictionary; witness the relation (a) of J. Franck's inquiry into the avatars of the word G. *Hexe* 'witch' to his Netherlandish dictionary and (b) of W. von Wartburg's experimental marshaling of the Romance names of the sheep (1918) — indisputably, a classic of its kind — to his distinctly later French etymological dictionary (*FEW*). In other instances the study of a single streak represents the modest *Gesellenstück* and the overall view of the given lexicon the subsequent *Meisterstück*. Thus, A. Ernout's doctoral dissertation (1909) on the dialectal ingredients of the Latin vocabulary was the logical forerunner of the ambitious all-embracing dictionary of Latin he compiled in later life (1932), in collaboration with A. Meillet; it also led, along a different path, to his lexicon of Umbrian (1961).

A readily understandable pattern of progress involves the gradual elaboration of an initial sketchy account into a full-blown, polished standard work which, in addition to its bolder scale, may also involve a more sweeping coverage. One thinks of the transmutation of a young S. Feist's modest *Grundriß der gotischen Etymologie* (1888), a slim book of fewer than two hundred pages, into the same scholar's definitive *Vergleichendes Wörterbuch der gotischen Sprache*, a monumental book of over seven hundred pages, via such intermediate stages as the two editions of his *Etymologisches Wörterbuch der gotischen Sprache* (1909, 1920-23). Similarly, A. Fick's very tentative *Wörterbuch der indogermanischen Grundsprache* (1868) underlies the three versions of his sprawling *Vergleichendes Wörterbuch der indogermanischen Sprachen* (1870-71, 1874-76, 1890-1909).

Given the affinity (indeed, mutual complementarity) of etymological and onomastic research, it is to be expected that the same mills are apt to grind out toponymic and anthroponymic dictionaries, aiming at a somewhat specialized readership, and general etymological dictionaries, of obviously wider appeal. G. Alessio came to the attention of scholars through his thick monograph on Calabrian toponymy (1939); subsequently he teamed up with a senior partner, C. Battisti, to produce the most comprehensive etymological dictionary of Italian (1950-57), and, while the latter venture was still in press, hastened back to the study of place names, concentrating this time on Greek toponyms in Sicily (1954-56). An indefatigable A. Dauzat went one step farther, cranking out not only a middle-sized etymological dictionary of French (1938) and, separately, an etymological dictionary of French first names and family names (1951) in addition to one — posthumously revised by Ch. Rostaing — of French place names (1963), but also two separate expository treatises on French toponymy (1926, 1930) as well as two separate presentations of French anthroponymy (1925, 1945) — quite apart from routine revisions and expansions in successive editions of some of these interconnected works. The analysis of a major corpus of onomastic material need not, of course, be explicitly organized as an etymological dictionary to qualify for consideration in this context: E. Gamillscheg's dictionary of French (1926) and his (preponderantly onomastic) study in early medieval migrations and settlements, *Romania Germanica* (1934-36), beautifully illustrate the mutual complementarity here posited.

It is equally easy to justify the pairing off of etymological and non-etymological ventures in lexicography. What ties them together, as experiences in scholarly work, is, clearly, not the distillation of genetic curiosity, but either the infatuation with certain techniques of lexicographic spadework or the commonness of scholarly habits their compilation presupposes (unless, of course, it is simply a sense of academic or civic responsibility). Examples are legion; two should suffice. M. B. Emeneau collaborated first with Dieter von den Steinen in manufacturing a Vietnamese- (or Annamese-) English dictionary — accompanied by an English-Vietnamese "Index" — (1945), and later teamed up with T. Burrow to produce *A Dravidian Etymological Dictionary* (1961). F. Holthausen authored, in his long life, as many as four different dictionaries explicitly labeled as "etymological" — presumably, a world record of endurance: one of modern English (1917), one of Old English (1934), one of Gothic (published that same year), and one — much delayed — of Old West Norse (1948). But he also specialized in making available non-etymological book-length dictionaries: one for Old Frisian (1925), the other for Old Saxon (1954), quite apart from editing — fully equipped with glossaries — the *Beowulf* and numerous other OE texts, analyzing place names (1929), editing Old Frisian glosses (1926), and engaging in many similar projects.

A discernibly different sort of combination, far more rewarding (one should think) in terms of scholarly enlightenment, is the "classic" split of a single thrust into two prongs: the historical grammar of a

given language (with special attention to phonology) and the etymological dictionary. For "unusual" languages a package of historical
grammar, glossary (often with etymological overtones), and sample
texts represented for decades a standard treatment; witness the books
by F. Justi (1864), J. Franck (1883), E. Berneker (1896), and
J. Endzelin (1922). In the case of better-known languages, where
maximum economy of resources was less imperative, grammar and
dictionary involved two separate stabs. Famous examples include, on
the Romance side, the fundamental syntheses by F. Diez and W.
Meyer-Lübke, which constitute the backbone of that speciality; and
one can cite equally celebrated instances of cleavage in the *œuvre* of
towering figures of Indo-European studies, starting with F. Bopp. In the
twentieth century the practice has become somewhat less common and
has certainly ceased to be nearly obligatory, as it at one moment
threatened to become; but cf. Emeneau and Burrow's slender *Dravidian
Comparative Phonology* (1970), modestly subtitled "a sketch," which
is easily identifiable as a by-product of their huge dictionary venture.

Is it relevant to raise the issue of how the project of an
etymological dictionary can be most advantageously fitted into the
lifework of a scholar? Without expatiating on a ticklishly personal
question, let me simply cite two extremes. The richly deserved,
unparalleled success of F. Kluge's *Etymologisches Wörterbuch der
deutschen Sprache* (traceable to the early 1880s), a classic of high-level
popularization at its most tasteful, is in no small part due to the
author's remarkable versatility. His own out-put includes major
inquiries into Proto-Germanic, into Finno-Germanic borrowings, into
paleo-Germanic nominal roots, into thieves' jargons, into the nautical
vocabulary, etc. With this kind of ceaseless self-immersion, over
decades, into ever new problems and of uninterrupted exposure to fresh
slices of illustrative material, Kluge could enrich and refine his
dictionary from one revised edition to another, in remarkably quick
succession. A sad counterexample, showing how not to go about the
task of compiling an etymological dictionary, was contributed by his
contemporary and compatriot, G. Körting (1891, 1901, 1907 for
comparative Romance, and 1908 for French). That fumbler wedged in
his twin projects between such totally unrelated massive enterprises as
the history of the English literature from oldest time, or the history of
the Greek and Roman theater. The results were *Machwerke* devoid of
any genuine value.

The problem of dual (or multiple) authorship of an etymological dictionary assumes a certain importance on account of the unavoidable admixture of strong doses of subjectivism to any variety of etymological decisions or solutions. An exaggerated neoromantic — not to say mystic — view of etymology (as professed in our own age by J. Corominas) would even favor the preparation and issuance of the various volumes comprising such a dictionary in extra-quick succession, so as to preserve the record of one inspired scholar's single panoramic vision of the field. Few level-headed experts share this extremist opinion slanted in the direction of subjectivity à outrance. There exist, as a matter of fact, several accepted forms of collaboration on a high level, starting with the revision of one aging or deceased expert's pronouncements by a younger worker. Such a situation may crystallize when a standard work is brought up to date for a new edition, witness J. B. Hofmann's very thorough recasting of A. Walde's classic Latin dictionary (1904-5, 1910) and A. Götze's (previously also W. Krause's and later A. Schirmer's and W. Mitzka's) excellent revision of the Kluge dictionary, to say nothing of Dubois and Mitterand's successful modernization of Dauzat's *DÉLF*. Under a different set of circumstances the reviser has deemed it more appropriate to add a supplement without tinkering with his predecessor's actual wording (cf. the relationship of A. Scheler to F. Diez in the refurbishing of the *EWRS*). It also happens that one etymologist, with a sharply pronounced scholarly personality, is invited to revise another's solutions and supporting arguments if the author originally entrusted with this task dies before the completion of the project; cf. the respective rôles of A. Darmesteter and A. Thomas, with regard to their etymological responsibilities, in the production of the *Dictionnaire général* and, above all, those of A. Walde and J. Pokorny in the delayed publication of the comparative IE dictionary. Then, two independently started dictionary projects may, at a certain juncture, be pooled, after the two authors learn about each other's designs, as happened, I understand, with Burrow and Emeneau's *DED*. Occasionally one man's small-scale dictionary ready for publication may profit from last-minute revision by another person — the author of a gradually maturing long-term project (O. Bloch vis-à-vis W. von Wartburg). Moving along a different axis, Wartburg, over a half-century of concentrated labor, developed a technique for inviting experts (e.g., V. Bertoldi, highly specialized as a glottobotanist) either to prepare individual entries in the field of their narrow competence, or to allow their privately furnished *ad hoc* interpretations to be quoted in full or in excerpts — quite apart from assigning practically the entire responsibility for whole volumes to hand-picked associates (H. E. Keller, P. Zumthor) and of securing the service of prestigious editorial assistants, some of them (such as J. Hubschmid) noted scholars in their own rights. There exist many other types of partnership (Alessio and Battisti, Dozy and Engelmann, Falk and Torp), not infrequently with an explicitly stated hierarchy in the chain of command (as when A. Duro clearly worked under the supervision of B. Migliorini). Under exceptional circumstances, a highly qualified translator was called upon to double up as a reviser (as is true of O. N. Trubačev vis-à-vis M. Vasmer). Possibly the single most arresting case of fruitful collaboration was, initially (1932), that between A. Ernout and his former mentor and long-time friend A. Meillet on the preparation of the *DÉLL,* inasmuch as each scholar examined practically every facet of each entry in a perspective germane to his expertise, placing it either in a strictly Latin ambiance or in an ambitiously wide IE context. In the revised editions (1939, etc.) Ernout eventually assumed full responsibility for both angles, just as Wartburg's share gradually crowded out that of O. Bloch, whom Wartburg outlived by a margin of over thirty years, in the consecutive editions of their *DÉLF.*

There exist, of course, numerous forms of lower-level collaboration, as when one self-effacing scholar volunteers to prepare an index for another's much-admired work (strictly speaking, C. Arendt, in 1863, indexed Bopp's comparative grammar rather than the *Altmeister's* dictionary, but the index, in any event, lends major etymological services; similarly, E. I. Hauschild's index to Diez's grammar and J. J. Jarník's index to the same founding father's dictionary both yield valuable clues to the etymological thinking of the scholar so honored). Modern examples are fairly numerous (e.g., H. Kuen vs. E. Gamillscheg or K. Reichardt vs. Walde and Pokorny or else H. B. Partridge vs. Pokorny's *IEW,* vol. II [1969]) and invite no discussion.

Among better-known varieties of informal collaboration one can adduce the critical reading of a virtually completed dictionary, just before it goes to press (as when J. Vendryes checked for accuracy the Celtic, especially Gaulish, bases in the Bloch-Wartburg *DÉLF*) or active help between fellow scholars or by a younger man to his former teacher, also vice versa, extended at the stage of galley proof corrections (Meyer-Lübke received such support when piloting his *REW* through choppy waters).

Aside from multifarious patterns of formal collaboration, there exist all kinds of deliberate "echoes," adaptations, and counterparts. As the subtitle ("histoire des mots") of Chantraine's Greek dictionary unmistakably shows, that work was calculated to be a pendant to Ernout-Meillet's Latin classic, within the framework of the same Parisian school.

Traditionally, an etymological dictionary is expected to appear either in the medium of the chosen language (thus, the natural thing to do is to select Hungarian as a vehicle for discussing the etymological subsoil of the lexicon of that language, cf. the case of Z. Gombocz and J. Melich) or in one of the "international languages" of organized scholarship, which for years were, indisputably, English, French, and German. Small wonder that for a language like Rumanian the ranking etymologists — all of them natives — had recourse either to their own tongue (Haşdeu, Candrea-Densusianu), or to German (Puşcariu), or to French (Cihac). On the other hand, only very bizarre political circumstances could have occasioned something as counterproductive as a dictionary of Rumanian word origins couched in Spanish (Cioranescu). Such was the prestige of German scholarship in historical and comparative linguistics before World War I that it amounted to more than just the peer of its principal rivals, French and English; thus, one understands that a dictionary like A. Tobler's *Altfranzösisches Wörterbuch* (not primarily etymological), planned before 1910, should have eventually started appearing in German garb, though the heir and reviser, E. Lommatzsch, might have had the foresight in the *inner bella* period to switch to French at the last moment. E. Gamillscheg used the lame excuse of writing his *EWFS* mainly for German teachers of French at the level of secondary education; but even this unconvincing explanation does not hold for Wartburg's *FEW*. For a comparative dictionary, such as Berneker's and Meyer-Lübke's, or a dead language, such as Hittite (cf. E. H. Sturtevant), the use of an international language has long been practically mandatory. For sentimental and practical reasons, a particularly meritorious dictionary addressed originally to a small, intimate circle of readers in a national language may ultimately reap the reward of fine scholarship by being translated into a widely understood medium (as happened to Falk and Torp's Norwegian-Danish venture, which eventually appeared in German; the respective dates are 1903-6 and 1910-11); or, conversely, the translation into the national language (posthumous in the case of M.

Vasmer's Russian Etymological Dictionary) may represent a kind of crowning achievement.

The unique success of F. Kluge's *EWDS* can be measured by the dual fact that, in addition to a straight translation into English from the fourth German edition (London, 1891), there also appeared, separately, an adaptation − by F. Lutz − to the needs of the student of English etymology (Boston, 1898) − understandably, an epitome phrased in English. To become a household word, an etymological dictionary had better be written in the relevant language; Skeat's dictionary of English may not have been the best available of its kind in the nineteenth century, but its counterparts couched in German could hardly compete with it in potential appeal to the English-speaking layman.

In this context it is perhaps advisable to hint at the graphemic aspect of etymological reference works. Precisely in deference to national cultural tranditions − conventional by definition − it is customary to use Greek script for the entries in an etymological dictionary of that language; Vasmer used Cyrillic letters both for the entries (in standard modern Russian) and for present-day Great Russian regionalisms, but had recourse to transliteration in citing Ukrainian, Byelorussian, Old Russian, Serbian, and Bulgarian cognates, to say nothing of his use of Latin letters for Sanskrit congeners. Similarly, E. König used Aramaic (i.e., standard Hebrew) script for Hebrew and Aramaic entries, but resorted to Latin transliteration in grappling with, say, Arabic counterparts. An alternative compromise between international symbolization and national tradition of spelling emerges in Mayrhofer's etymological dictionary of Sanskrit, where the script is consistently Latin, but the sequence of letters in the entries (A-M) throughout the two volumes so far available betrays adherence to a widely accepted local arrangement.

The status of graphemics is entirely different in such etymological dictionaries as involve ancient cultures geared to ideo- or logographs. As Paul L.-M. Serruys has pointed out in his searching review (1973) of Chang Hsüan's *The Etymologies of Three Thousand Chinese Characters* ... (1968), there exists in Far Eastern studies a subdiscipline which deserves to be set apart, the "etymology of characters", which fundamentally bears on the relation between graphs and words.[2]

19

2

TIME DEPTH

As regards choice and implications of the ideal time depth, the thinking of tone-setting etymologists has undergone considerable changes; nevertheless, there remains ample room for further improvement. It is clear to everyone that one must select a well-defined starting point along the time axis, which may correspond to the present-day state of a language (modern West Armenian, say), or to a — culturally, structurally, or developmentally — conspicuous past stage of a language still in use today (e.g., Homeric Greek), or to a language completely extinct, but one of which there exists a corpus (such as Tocharian A), or to a dead language of unquestionable authenticity but one that completely lacks written attestation (colloquial Afro-Latin, as once used in Numidia). It is further clear that, from the present, one is free to move only backward, while from a point in the past one is free to move in either direction. The unsolved question is, How far is it advisable or permissible for the etymologist to move along the time axis?

One may start the discussion by describing practices that have been resolutely abandoned and that seem to stem from a romantic infatuation with the distant past. When Bolza, a year or so before the appearance of Diez's comparative Romance dictionary (*EWRS*), published his "genetic-etymological dictionary" of Italian, he not only arranged for ancestral bases (Latin, Greek in transliteration, modern German as a substitute for paleo-Germanic, and classical Arabic) to function as the actual entries, but he added parenthetically to these bases also their cognates, as assumed a century and a quarter ago — thus *acer, aeger, aes, cellō, celō, cēnseō* are flanked by Sanskrit congeners, *aer* and *aestus* are accompanied by Greek and Sanskrit relatives, for *rapiō* and *rancidus* Germanic counterparts are provided, the hazy, inexplicit implication of all this being the projection of the respective words onto the unspecified time level of an "Ursprache." Three decades later, R. Barcia, in his five-volume pioneering dictionary of Spanish, made a compromise with common sense by listing as entries the modern Spanish end results of the lexical trajectories, but needlessly stuffed his reference work with all kinds of irrelevant bits of information (on Italian, French, dialectal French, Provençal, and Catalan cognates of the entries and on the Greek counterparts of the

Latin bases invoked, cf. s.v. *capra* 'goat'), spicing the whole exhibit with specimens of Greek and Arabic (if no longer of Sanskrit) script; and while his immediate successor E. de Echegaray diluted and compressed this lavish information on remote antecedents, viewed through the prism of cognates, there remain enough superfluities in his compilation (1887-89) to invite energetic pruning.[1]

How far, then, should one defensibly go back in retrospective analysis? From the vantage of pure, unbiased scholarship a perfect temporal span would involve just one step back, and this schema is, under certain circumstances, applicable, as when in the book-sized glossary to a medieval Romance text the immediately underlying etyma (Latin, Frankish, Gothic, Arabic) are provided; witness W. Foerster's Chrétien vocabulary, Menéndez Pidal's long-authoritative *Cid* vocabulary, and H. B. Richardson's less impressive, but not incompetently executed, etymological guide to Juan Ruiz. However, an etymological dictionary of modern French, normally planned as a commercial venture, would, predictably, entail economic failure, if the reader were to be gently led from mid-twentieth-century words to their, let us assume, early-eleventh-century prototypes, despite the undeniable scholarly advantages, in terms of rigor, of such a modest delimitation. The reason for this state of affairs is that familiarity with medieval French carries with it, in the Old World, distinctly smaller prestige than does the command of classical Latin and Greek. The exacting user expects the seasoned etymologist to lend him his hand on an intellectual safari through time leading toward a prestigious goal, where his thirst for knowledge may be quenched. On this matter, there has been complete unanimity of opinion between the pioneers Brachet, Clédat, Scheler, and their successors down to Bloch, Dauzat, and the latter's disciples; at best an experienced, sophisticated etymologist will agree to list the Old French form as a mid-point between the start and the finish, as do, indeed, with praiseworthy deftness, Mitterand and Dubois in their revision of Dauzat's *DÉLF.*

The situation is slightly different in the Germanic domain, inasmuch as neither Middle High German nor Old High German happens to be a fully collegiate or prestige language of any particular importance or appeal to the layman. In a historical dictionary that is only incidentally etymological, such as Betz's masterly revision (1960) of Paul's *Deutsches Wörterbuch,* one will find at strategic points brief references to OHG and MHG usage; also an occasional discreet hint of the "common Germanic" character of a lexical family; and, at rare intervals, bare allusions to Gothic and Scandinavian preferences or to correspondences in the better-known IE cognate languages (particularly Latin), with strict avoidance of any ostentatious display of etymological erudition, such as one might have taken for granted in a representative nineteenth-century compilation.

Overt prospective collections of etymological equations involving short timespans are rare. But the compiler of a glossary to, say, Chaucer's works supplies such a collection — conceivably without intending to do so — simply by providing modern English glosses. Where there has occurred no major shift in meaning and where basically the same words, albeit in slightly different garb, serve both as the entry and the gloss, one can easily cull a whole etymological miniature dictionary from such a strictly exegetic glossary.

Conversely, one encounters, in advanced etymology, very sophisticated spatio-temporal edifices. For one early example of intricate structure take Berneker's comparative Slavic dictionary — unfortunately, left a torso (1908-13). The author spreads out his material under an alphabetically-arranged succession of Proto-Slavic entries, all of which, by definition, involve reconstructions, so that the raised asterisk, as the common denominator of their hypothetic status, can be altogether dispensed with; the author's broad policies of reconstruction, which on eight scores happen to differ from those of his immediate predecessor Franz Miklosich (1886), are explicitly stated in an introductory remark. The first tier of a typical entry includes a procession of Slavic products, marshaled in a prearranged conventional sequence: Old Church Slavic, then, almost clockwise: Russian, Ukrainian, Byelorussian, Bulgarian, Serbocroatian, etc. (note the absence of Macedonian, which lacked an independent rank sixty years ago). The genetic discussion is deliberately kept at a minimum. A second tier is reserved for the integration of the fine-meshed Slavic evidence with the necessarily coarse-meshed IE material, offered selectively: with Sanskrit representing Indo-Aryan, Avestan standing for Iranian, Latin for Italic, and Irish for Celtic. Since the link of most Slavic families with their distant relatives is incomparably more subject to caution than are the intra- and inter-Slavic connections, the tone of the exposition changes abruptly, allowing for the presentation and laconic assessment of conflicting hypotheses. Where serious problems of adjudication arise on the Slavic level, a mezzanine floor, as it were, is constructed, so as to relieve for those readers who reach out for the second tier most of their doubts bearing on the Slavic material.

Berneker's dictionary must, up to a certain point, have served as a model for the Ernout-Meillet classic, except that, instead of a single virtuoso performer deftly changing rôles in each entry, we can here observe and applaud the splendid coordination of two minds. Ernout's task is confined to presenting a single language in all its scintillating complexity, a limitation which allows him to do three things that were unattainable for Berneker: to scrutinize each lexical family in all its derivational and compositional ramifications; to pay adequate attention, at every step, to denotations and even to connotations; and to distinguish as meticulously as the texts allow between archaic, Republican, early Imperial, and Late Antiquity usages, with further allowance for a rich palette of social dialects and regional (provincial) preferences. Temporally, Ernout is concerned, in well-attested families, with an 800- to 900-year segment; and, before bowing out, he reports as carefully as his rapidly obsolescent sources (e.g., Meyer-Lübke's *REW*, unrevised since 1935) enable him to do, on the survival of each chosen Latin word in Romance, Celtic, Germanic, and/or Slavic. Where he leaves off, Meillet, in a smooth change of guard, takes over, exposing the reader to Greek, Armenian, Hittite evidence, etc. — a breath-taking spatial sweep which also implies an equally bold temporal plunge — in the direction of Proto-IE. With Ernout pushing us forward and Meillet pulling us backward, we are privileged to enjoy an unprecedented panoramic view of a major slice of the IE lexicon.

For one unusual extension of the customary time span — indeed, a kind of leap — one may turn to certain varieties of substratum research. The familiar succession of events — supported by historiographic and archaeological evidence — prompts one to set off two successive processes in and around the Western Mediterranean: (a) the infiltration of "substratal" words (many of them pre-IE) into standard or provincial Latin, and (b) their further drifting, as more or less thoroughly assimilated ingredients of the Latin lexicon, into the daughter languages. Operationally, however, it is not invariably feasible to segment this long-drawn-out process into two neatly-delimited phases, because Latin documentation happens not to be at all times readily available. All too often, the earliest traces of the putative primeval bases that one detects or distills are medieval place-names ferreted out in obscure charters and/or modern regionalisms. Research along this line — inherently hazardous and time-consuming — has been advancing at a slow pace, with a few daredevils inching forward, typically from one monograph to another. But J. Hubschmid, currently the most heavily committed devotee of this approach, has announced and, in fact, launched a series titled *Thesaurus Praeromanicus,* which points in the direction of a forthcoming etymological dictionary so slanted.[2] The distance between base and product may in this domain run to several millennia.

Aside from these problems of macrochronology — the patterns of major divisions — there are those of microchronology, which bear on individual word histories, as traced within the framework of a dictionary. In the older ventures, such lexical vignettes were, practically, unaccompanied by morsels of chronological information; as regards English, this is particularly true of the original edition (1882) of Skeat's meritorious thesaurus. Approximately forty years later the popularizer E. Weekley liberalized this attitude of rigid aloofness, interspersing the entries with absolute dates of "first appearances" where historical circumstances so warranted (s.vv. *ducat* and *farad,* say), or with relative datings (*grandson* came long after *grandfather*), or with a combination of both (*governance* [Wyclif] preceded *government* [sixteenth century]). In most instances, however, the rough date of emergence is implied in the source, as when the author traces *drone, drop, dross, fair, fall* to Old English, but *disdain, disgorge, disguise,* and *disgust* to Old French, and one notes a consistent lack of enlightenment on all learned formations, whichever their itineraries and eventual ports of entry (*diploma, dubious,* etc.). E. Klein's dictionary, despite the recency of its publication (1966-67), unfortunately marks a return to the antiquated practice of Skeat, but there has at long last become available to the researcher, as if by compensation, a straight *Chronological English Dictionary,* by a team of Continental workers (T. Finkenstaedt et al.), which lists as many as 80,000 words in order of their earliest verifiable occurrence.

The evolutionary line is much tidier in the field of French lexicography. Here the watershed corresponds, *grosso modo,* to the year 1930. Over against the older compilations (Brachet, Clédat, Scheler, Gamillscheg), almost wholly indifferent to the matter of dating, stand the younger dictionaries (Bloch and Wartburg, Dauzat-Dubois-Mitterand) which, however economical in other respects, as a rule never neglect the two dimensions of date and meaning. The Bloch dictionary, time and again, specifies not only the writers' first, tentative tinkering with a word ("une première fois . . ."), but also its definitive introduction, reminding us that word histories, at their early stages at least, deserve to be symbolized by dotted rather than solid lines, on account of the intermittent character of the transmission of most items (as is particularly true of "waves" of Latinisms and Hellenisms). The major improvement in French is due, in part, to the fairly quick publication of Wartburg's *FEW*, in part to the good performance of a few younger workers specializing in "Vordatierungen." The feature that is still almost entirely missing, despite the explicit theoretical recognition — in many quarters — of the need for it, is the listing of *last* occurrences, which it should be relatively easy to catch with the aid of appropriately programmed computers.

Despite the fundamental differences between historical and etymological dictionaries, a gradual transition is conceivable along the temporal axis. Suppose the historical dictionary is so architectured (R. J. Cuervo's *Diccionario de construcción y régimen* is a case in point) that the oldest uses are recorded toward the very end of an elaborate documentary section constituting the core of each entry, with the last illustration corresponding to the earliest actual occurrence; and that one finds, appended to the documentation, a succinctly stated etymological solution. Within this particular arrangement, the oldest examples of the "daughter language" flow into the record of the parent language, a remarkably smooth link-up.

3

THE DIRECTION OF CHANGE

Time depth and direction of change are so intimately interwoven that some of the remarks relevant to the latter have already been made in the discussion of the former; one hesitates to repeat them. It is vital to remember that on the commercial market only retrospective etymological dictionaries command attention; their prospective counterparts are for "initiates" alone. A technically many-splendored dictionary like W. von Wartburg's *FEW* and Bolza's clumsy "genetic" dictionary of Italian are, in this respect, similar and not unlike G. Gröber's celebrated collection of reconstructed Vulgar Latin bases ("Lateinische Substrate romanischer Wörter").

As regards the history of philological scholarship, one notes the priority of the retrospective approach. Outside etymology, Nebrixa could afford to work bidirectionally by compiling both a Spanish-Latin and a Latin-Spanish vocabulary. But the early etymologists invariably started out from the later stage — typically, their own mother tongue. Rosal and Covarrubias tried to dig a tunnel from seventeenth-century Spanish to Latin (Greek, Arabic, Hebrew, etc.), and Ménage, a few decades later, proceeded similarly — *mutatis mutandis* — with French; to neither would it have occurred to start out from Latin (and other ancestral languages) and to work toward his favorite vernacular. When comparatists, such as Berneker and Meyer-Lübke, much later used the reversed perspective, they still started, at the preliminary stage, with the products (Slavic, Romance) of the evolutions surveyed, but did not bother to initiate their readers into that preparatory phase of the operation.

One notable drawback of the retrospective view has long been known to authors and experienced users, but may never have been thrashed out in formal discussion. Suppose the book at issue is an etymological dictionary of modern French; such delimitation allows the etymologist in charge to retrieve only one part of the immensely rich Old French vocabulary, namely those ingredients that have survived — centrally or marginally — into Classical and modern French. Very often, however, the clinching argument in the relevant etymological analysis will hinge on certain words (derivatives, compounds, synonyms, homonyms, antonyms, and the like) that no longer form part of the French lexicon. The ill-fated author of such a dictionary has the uncomfortable choice between indulging in excursuses outside the self-imposed scope of his lexicographic venture (as E. Gamillscheg has not infrequently done in his *EWFS* and, especially, J. Corominas in his *DCE*) or cutting short the analysis at its most tantalizing point. Alternatively, the reader may feel that a prospective and a retrospective dictionary, being mutually complementary, should habitually be used side by side. As a matter of fact, V. García de Diego's *DEEH* represents an attempt — poorly executed, but in principle noteworthy — to offer the reader two such interdependent dictionaries between two covers. In most contexts, all that can be accomplished is the compilation of a cross-index, as when Meyer-Lübke appended to his *REW*, which supplies ancestral bases, a rather elaborate master index of Romance forms.

Just as considerations of pragmatism and practicality have had their share of influence on retrospective etymological dictionaries alone, so prospective dictionaries boast, as one of their distinctive features, a heavy commitment to comparatism. If one ascends from a "daughter language" to an ancestral tongue (real or hypothetical), comparative data, provided they are judiciously doled out, remain an accessory, while otherwise tending to become a mere frill. The reverse temporal projection carries with it the reader's expectation of witnessing the splitting of a — more or less homogeneous — "parent language" into a sizable number of "daughter languages," an expectation whetting that same reader's hunger for comparative analysis, and ultimately rooted in the traditional family-tree projection, proven wrong on so many occasions, yet never fully replaced by a viable alternative. The archetypal prospective dictionary, ineradicably comparative, remains one that starts out from reconstructed Proto-IE, such as Walde-Pokorny's bold venture, characteristically titled *Vergleichendes Wörterbuch der indogermanischen Sprachen* (1927-32) — here comparatism implies etymological digging — or Pokorny's own *IEW* (1948-69).

The fact that the commercially sponsored majority of retrospective dictionaries have to take into account the layman's involvement has contributed to the widely held opinion that a dictionary, being a reference work by definition, is hardly the ideal testing ground for bold ideas with respect to methods and conjectures, but merely, at best, a convenient depository of knowledge painstakingly distilled elsewhere. Most etymological discoveries are, obviously, made in articles and notes; a few can be culled from historical grammars and textual annotations, including glossaries appended to meticulous philological editions of older texts. These minor genres do not actually compete with full-fledged etymological dictionaries in terms of handiness, massiveness of documentation, etc. There do exist, however, book-length studies — often equipped with indexes, bibliographies, and the remaining paraphernalia of a scholarly apparatus — each concerned with a string of representative etymological problems included in the assortment because the author apparently felt that the moment had arrived to ventilate them. Such loosely-organized, but by no means loosely-argued, monographs are exemplified, on a high level of scholarship, by A. Meillet's *Études sur l'étymologie et le vocabulaire du vieux slave* (1904-5). Studies so planned (and obligatorily channeled through strictly academic series) afford the writers incomparably greater freedom of maneuvering, are compatible with a light topical bias, and can ultimately be called upon to nourish a more conventionally organized dictionary, whose compiler is, inversely, understood to shy away from the mere hint of lopsidedness.

4
RANGE

If languages — and words forming part of their respective vocabularies — actually followed in their courses the simple rectilinear trajectories postulated by Schleicher, then the author of an etymological dictionary of, say, Gothic would have to reach just one major decision: whether to stop short at providing a Proto-Germanic etymon for each word used by Wulfila or to go beyond that modest goal and aim at furnishing a Proto-IE "root." A skeletal etymological glossary could indeed be so parsimoniously organized, but would, as a result of the economy achieved, be unenlightening; after all, qualified readers make a point of looking for justification of every etymological gambit, so paleo-Germanic evidence, in addition to the given Gothic form or forms, must be adduced to vindicate the author's Proto-Germanic reconstruction, and the remaining IE languages must be appealed to in any search for even more remote ancestral bases. Inevitably, then, any explicative, as against purely referential, etymological dictionary will become broadly comparative, even if a single language remains designedly at the center of attention. Thus there crystallizes the slightly paradoxical genre of a comparative dictionary of, overtly, just one language, much as there exists, independently, a comparative historical grammar confined to a single evolutionary span.[1] Interestingly, L. Diefenbach published as early as 1851 the two volumes of his *Vergleichendes Wörterbuch der gotischen Sprache.* In our own century, S. Feist — who had modestly started out, in his early twenties, with a slender *Grundriß der gotischen Etymologie* (1888) — produced in his prime a bolder and not so slim *Etymologisches Wörterbuch* of Gothic (1909), recast that middle-sized dictionary thoroughly (1920-23), then, in his old age, succumbed to the temptation of labeling its definitive version (1939) *Vergleichendes Wörterbuch* of Gothic, thus practically reverting to Diefenbach's old dream. In the process of its successive revisions and expansions, Feist's own book grew from 167 to 738 pages.

It is stimulating to watch an expert of Feist's caliber at work. Let us select the 1923 phase of his favorite project — removed by exactly a half-century from our own observation post — when it was past its midpoint. From the seasoned etymologist's Preface we learn that he was convinced of the relevance of Tocharian, but not yet of the wisdom of having recourse to Hittite. With the help of friends as highly specialized as R. Thurneysen (Celtic), N. van Wijk (Slavic and Baltic), F. Holthausen (Old English and Frisian), and W. Siegling (Tocharian), he tapped an extraordinary amount of resources: not only the full orchestra of Germanic languages (including such obscure members of the family as Old East Frankish, Dithmarsian spoken at the western coast of Schleswig-Holstein, and Gutnian, an archaic Swedish dialect confined to Gotland − a particularly "functional" cognate), not only the nearly-complete range of other IE languages, with full attention to Celtic, to numerous Greek dialects, and to Iranian tongues as esoteric as Balochi and Ossetic, but even Basque, Chaldaic, Estonian, Georgian, Karian, Livian, and Sumerian. Of course, most of these peripheral languages came in merely for incidental or oblique mention as the discussion of each entry, starting in low gear with the austere delineation of inflection, affixation, and composition within Gothic and with the tidy identification of meanings through appeal to New Testament Greek equivalents, gradually acquired momentum through the marshaling, first, of more provocative pan-Germanic and, second, of decidedly conjectural IE evidence, part of the latter being intertwined − through diffusion − with the records of non-IE languages. Feist's blueprint for Germanic resembles, then, Berneker's for Slavic, except that the entries this time are no longer reconstructions and that one member of the family is programmatically favored over the others. Ironically, Feist happened to adopt a skeptical attitude toward the reconstruction of "roots," deliberately using small print for their discussion and, in most instances, downright rejection. Thus, the heavy scaffolding of comparative support was no longer justified by so much as the writer's confidence in the scholarly world's ability to engage persuasively in any long-range, "sweeping" reconstruction.

While Feist's − by no means extravagant − attitude is a dramatic reminder that "tout se tient" in etymology, so that Tocharianists are bound to benefit from progress in Gothic studies just as the reverse has been proven true, it is nevertheless a fact that the range of an etymological dictionary, defined as the number or sum of languages principally taken into account in genetic operations, up to a certain point remains under the compiler's control. One discerns certain typical recurrent situations; to describe them, it is useful to distinguish with particular neatness between source languages and target languages.

A good illustration of multifurcation at the source is provided by the unique genre of a German *Fremdwörterbuch,* whatever one may think of the cultural climate of intolerance and xenophobia in which such ventures thrive. One such classic, oft-revised and brought up to date at least as late as 1903, is the [*Allgemeines verdeutschendes und erklärendes*] *Fremdwörterbuch* by the pioneer J. C. A. Heyse (1764-1829). While the implication of such a dictionary may be puristic, remedial, and even *kulturpolitisch,* its execution need not be incompetent, and its etymological, as against its therapeutic, component may be perfectly sound. Here we have a multiplicity of sources, typically involving languages − whether dead or living − of high prestige, such as Greek, Latin, French, and English, and a single target, namely German. The etymological operation hardly goes beyond winnowing out what is allegedly alien to the German, or rather Germanic, native tradition (*Erbgut*).

Radically different in overtones, but not necessarily in etymological architecture, are such dictionaries as promise to account for all sorts of picturesque exoticisms converging upon a single modern language. Dictionaries so slanted, varying as to seriousness of purpose, appeal to readers, and merit of professional workmanship, exist for practically every European language. The archetype is, conceivably, M. Devic's *Dictionnaire des mots français d'origine orientale* (1876) − which stressed Arabic, but transcended it, including Malay (in addition to Hebrew, Persian, and Turkish). The Spanish intellectuals' traditional, almost innate, concern with the Moorish strain of their native culture justifies the strikingly early date (1886) of the appearance of L. Eguílaz y Yanguas' *Glosario etimológico de las palabras españolas . . . de origen oriental.* Unfortunately, the book is bizarre at both ends of the etymological axis: With respect to source languages, its dependence on Devic is embarrassingly close (Eguílaz included Malay, a language he knew far less thoroughly than did his predecessor, but neglected Indo-Aryan, this despite his acquaintance with Sanskrit), and at the receiving end he made a point of citing all the languages of the Peninsula, down to Basque, among the beneficiaries! The German counterpart that comes to mind first would be, in tribute to the author's reputation as Orientalist, Enno Littmann's *Morgenländische Wörter im Deutschen* (1920); less understandable is the fact that the revised second edition (1924) should have been enriched − in response to public demand or as a bow to the publisher's pressure? − by a supplement on words of indigenous American stock, where Littmann had to tread unfamiliar ground. It is, of course, not necessary for books of this kind to serve the interests of a single country by catering to the speakers of just one language. K. Lokotsch, for instance, organized his Americanistic etymological dictionary (1926) so as to take into account ("mit steter Berücksichtigung") English, Spanish, and French alongside German; the following year, he expanded his program in offering a dictionary of European words of Oriental ancestry, with explicit inclusion of Germanic, Romance, and Slavic on the side of target languages. Here we witness a complete departure from Devic's model: There is a deliberately-chosen multiplicity of target languages, though it does not remotely balance the enormous wealth of source languages. Perhaps the major consideration was to increase the usefulness and, consequently, the circulation of the book. One suspects a similar motive on the part of Georg Friederici, *Hilfswörterbuch für den Amerikanisten* (1926), whose lexicon mediates between autochthonous New World languages and a mixed group of German-, Spanish-, and English-oriented readers. Friederici, incidentally, unlike Littmann and Lokotsch, was a bona fide guide to American antiquities ("Erklärungen altertümlicher Ausdrücke"), which he knew at first hand from a quarter-century of specialized research. Interestingly, he spoke of "Lehnwörter aus Indianersprachen," while Heyse (and Heyse's peers) had rallied to defend German from the invasion of "Fremdwörter"; nobody would want to eliminate words as innocuous and, at the same time, irreplaceably specific as *Kanu* 'canoo.'

Over against these practical considerations, target languages may be arrayed on purely historical grounds. W. H. Engelmann very wisely classed Spanish with Portuguese in his trail-blazing glossary of Arabisms (1861), and A. Steiger, whose *Contribución* (1932) is not, strictly, an etymological dictionary but can, with a measure of flexibility, be used as one, went one step farther and accorded equal status to Spanish, Portuguese, Catalan, Sicilian. The next logical advance (attempted by G. B. Pellegrini in 1972) was in the direction of a pan-Romanic study of Arabisms.

Most of the books here listed serve to satisfy the curiosity of the educated layman, the *littérateur,* or of the scholar — be he historian, geographer, or anthropologist — only indirectly concerned with etymological niceties. Certainly, it is not R. Dozy's modest pioneering pamphlet on Orientalisms (*Oosterlingen*) in Netherlandish (i.e., on words of Arabic, Hebrew, Chaldaic = Aramaic, Persian, and Turkish background) — a booklet that actually preceded Devic's venture by a margin of nine years — which sealed the Dutch Semitologist's reputation, but weightier volumes, such as his *Dictionnaire détaillé des noms des vêtements chez les Arabes* (1845) and, even more, his *Supplément aux dictionnaires arabes* (1881). But certain books of this kind must be taken seriously: the 32-page bibliography appended to Pellegrini's two-volume project lends it the dimension of a monograph, while R. Lenz's *Diccionario etimológico de las voces chilenas derivadas de lenguas indígenas americanas* remains, despite the strictures of younger critics (Jorge Suárez, for one), the most significant, erudite, and sophisticated contribution to a field intrinsically difficult of access. Here the etymological dictionary really, for once, becomes the laboratory — not merely a storehouse for knowledge acquired elsewhere.

Within Europe, the sharp division of a language into different etymological strains has been cultivated mainly with regard to Rumanian. Rumanian has, since the founding of organized linguistic research, equally fascinated Romanists (Diez, Schuchardt) and students of Southeastern Europe (Miklosich); several etymological dictionaries reflect in their grand design this cleavage, opposing the Latin heritage to the sum of all non-Latin sources, a very mixed bag indeed (cf. A. de Cihac's two volumes [1870-79] as well as the torsos of S. Puşcariu's [1905] and Candrea and Densusianu's [1907-14] projects).

There exist other special, even unique, situations. One of them prevails in the case of Old Testament dictionaries, of which the better (W. Gesenius, E. König) carry a modicum of etymological information. Since a minor part of the OT happens to be phrased in Biblical Aramaic, it is customary — and, from the theologian's point of view, entirely justified — to have the two source languages, Hebrew and Aramaic, lumped together.

In addition to the familiar type of comparative etymological dictionary — the one which examines, under a magnifying glass, relationships between languages already known to be cognate — there exists the rare reconnoitering type of etymological glossary, whose purpose is to explore the possibility or wisdom of a rapprochement. Take the development of Karl Bouda: branching out from his article "Baskisch und Kaukasisch" (1948), which in turn goes back to a pioneering monograph (less sharply polarized), *Die Beziehungen des Sumerischen zum Baskischen, Westkaukasischen und Tibetischen* (1938), Bouda finally achieved the summit of originality in such slim booklets bursting with new ideas as *Baskisch-kaukasische Etymologien* (1949) — a neatly-wrapped package of 218 additional lexical correspondences — and, three years later, *Neue baskisch-kaukasische*

Etymologien. In the aggregate, these very bold researches have been pointing toward a future Basque-Georgian (or Ibero-Caucasian) comparative dictionary, on the assumption that a certain validity attaches to the hypothesis of the kinship thus postulated. It has taken the interplay of several factors to make this audacious research possible. As A. Martinet remarked in his unusually flattering review almost a quarter-century ago (*Word*, VII, 279-82), Bouda owes a heavy debt to René Lafon's concurrent researches, principally to the Frenchman's article "Concordances morphologiques entre le basque et les langues caucasiques," whose importance stems from Lafon's superb command of the morphology of the older Basque verb (1943). Lafon himself advanced, in his search for affinities, from inflection to derivation, a step which of course brought him closer to etymology ("Sur un suffixe nominal commun au basque et à quelques langues caucasiques," *BSLP,* XLIV [1947-48], 144-54). Bouda brought to the task, as his personal share, an uncommon versatility and a fertile imagination, as shown by his doctoral research in Ob-Ugrian (1933), by his studies in Basque phytonymy (1955), by his exploration of possible kinship between the languages of the Kamchadals, the Koryaks (= Nymylyans), and the Chukchi in northeastern Siberia, also by an occasional safari into a little-known variety of Caucasian: *Lakkische Studien* (1949). If one adopts a cyclic view of scholarship, one may foresee a comparative grammar emerging from Bouda's pioneering etymological pamphlets and, as the next phase, the appearance of a full-blown etymological dictionary.

Should the formally announced target language be, strictly, the terminal point in the dimensions of time and space? Not necessarily so, in the hands of a deft and balanced etymologist. In this respect, the *Oxford Dictionary of English Etymology* (1966) has set an enviable record of flexibility. Despite severe limitations on space, Onions and his associates have succeeded not only in placing English at the receiving end in the line stretching from Med. L. *Pamphilus (de amore)* through OFr. (beside MDu.) *Pamphilet ~ Panflet* to E. *pamphlet* (~ Anglo-L. *panfletus*), but also in identifying mod. E. as the source of Fr. *pamphlet* and the latter, in turn, as the immediate model of G. *Pamphlet.* In other instances, where the web of relationships cannot yet be stated quite so categorically, the Onions team wisely resorts to a looser formulation. Thus, E. *pandemonium* is a transparent Hellenism, and the record shows that it was funneled into the vernaculars through Late Latin. The Romance languages exhibit several cognates, including Fr.

pandémonium (in Voltaire, *-ion*) and Sp. It. *pandemonio*. One cannot possibly determine without applying the finest lenses whether all these forms have been separately bequeathed by Dying Antiquity or whether there occurred a certain osmosis between, say, French and English, or Italian and Spanish literary usages; Onions lists these forms, but leaves the issue of their interconnection provisionally open. In the case of *pandora* 'string musical instrument of the cither type' it would have sufficed, for the Oxford dictionary's avowed prime purpose, to reconstruct the line Gr. *pandoûra* → Late L. *pandūra* → It. *pand-ura*, *-ora* → E. *pandora*, but Onions, judiciously, smuggles in the information that Fr. *pandore* was also minted in imitation of the Italian model word, thus evoking, with a few strokes of the pen, the climate of a whole musical era: *pandora* becomes a European "period piece." The space needed for such tangential remarks has been provided by occasional restraints from elaboration at other levels, as when Gr. *pandoûra* is evasively classed: "Probably of Oriental origin," without the ventilation of any risky hypotheses involving the dawn of history.

In addition to national languages, there has developed, especially over the last two centuries, an international language of science which, by and large, involves translucid Greek and Latin etyma, with slight adaptations, in each country, to local spelling habits. Given the triviality of the differences, there may be room, in the near future, for an etymological dictionary of science (or of the sciences), for which multilingual terminological glossaries — such as those that Marouzeau and, after him, Rose Nash and others have compiled for modern linguistics — may serve as feeders.

Meanwhile, we have to decide how much information a nationally-slanted etymological dictionary should convey about the technical international vocabulary. One important criterion is the vitality of the given term as an ingredient of the national culture and its linguistic vehicle. Do there exist abbreviations, of the type familiar from E. *telly* (Fr. *télé*) 'television', E. *polio* 'poliomyelitis, infantile paralysis' and *T.B.* 'tuberculosis'? Has the word at issue cast off derivatives, entered into compounds, contributed to the rise of stereotyped phrases, left traces of a peculiar semantic development, produced any impact on phonotactics and morphotactics? Or does it drift through the lexicon of the host language as an unassimilated corpuscle?

Just how wide the leeway remains in editorial decisions of this type is made clear by comparison of two fairly recent etymological dictionaries of modern Italian (incidentally, both traceable to Florence): C. Battisti and G. Alessio go to the extreme of recording in their *DEI* not only the bound form *cranio-* and the nearly identical free form *crànio*, but also, under the former entry, *cranio-cerebrale, -facciale* [hybrid rather than learned!], *-faringèo, -timpànico;* and, separately, *craniocèle, -clasìa, -claste, -gnòmica, -grafìa, -grafo, -ìde, -lària, -òlogo, -mante, -manzìa, -metro, -pago, -patìa, -schisi, -scopo, -stenòsi,* etc. G. Devoto, a more level-headed scholar bent on economy, is satisfied, in his slightly later *Avviamento*, with listing the primitive *cranio* plus the "lean" family *cranio-logìa, -metrìa, -scopìa, -tomìa,* with the briefest of comments.

5

GRAND STRATEGY: THE TOTAL ORGANIZATION OF THE CORPUS

While the array of entries in a single alphabetic sequence has unquestionably become the standard procedure, despite a few startling exceptions (see below), the intricate problems of alphabetization and cross-referencing have not yet been completely solved. Some of these difficulties are old; they are due to the authors' striving for economy and compactness, and they also reflect these authors' (or their publishers') tentative assessment of the experience and sophistication of the average, better still, of the ideal, readers.

Thus, in the original edition (1882) of Skeat's classic dictionary one finds countless references — occasionally accompanied by crisp qualifying remarks — from variant forms, including variant spellings, to the respective main entries, such as from *miniver* to *meniver*, from *munnion* ("the older and correct form") to *mullion*, from *mustache, mustachio* to *moustache*; where the first letters of two competing forms happen to be identical, a single composite entry suffices: *nankeen, nankin.* The revised 1909 edition followed the same pattern in its intercalated addenda: *mongoose,* see *mungoose,* and corrected a sprinkling of earlier omissions, by providing, e.g., a cross-reference from *mirky* to *murky,* where the earlier text was satisfied with listing *murky, mirky.* Problems in consulting Skeat arise with words like *mumps:* If it derives from *mump,* as the author asserts, should the two items have been consolidated? On the whole, Skeat's etymological "style" favored a multitude of separate, autonomous entries with a profusion of cross-references, some of which, by today's standard, seem otiose. One is surprised to be specifically reminded, under the pretext of very thin genetic threads, of *mortal,* s.v. *murrain;* of *mouse,* s.v. *muscle;* of *muzzle,* s.v. *muse* (verb); of *moss,* s.v. *mushroom;* of *mire,* s.v. *moss;* and of *mud,* s.v. *mother* 'lees': The dictionary, in an age of relative leisure, obviously served as a substitute for a series of "chatty" lectures. And the unbridled enthusiasm for "roots" added to the prolixity: s.v. *mutilate* the author would draw the reader's attention to *minish* ("probably from $\sqrt{}$ MA or MI"); s.v. *mythology* the reader would be exposed to an excursus on the possible relation of Gr. $\mu\tilde{\upsilon}\theta o\varsigma$ via $\mu\tilde{\upsilon}$ 'slight sound,' 'word, saying' to E. *mum* (which also gratuitously haunts the entry *mutter*), all of them allegedly traceable to $\sqrt{}$ MU.

But even with a thoroughly up-to-date dictionary, such as the revised fourth edition (1959-60) of Ernout and Meillet's *DÉLL,* an extensive training period is required if the reader is to extract from it the maximum of useful, meticulously distilled information. The salient feature of the *DÉLL* is the consistent subsumption of most lexical units, except for certain isolated débris left adrift, under word families; the reader is expected to be in a position to "peel off" from a word, on whose provenience he seeks enlightenment, the affixes and to make into the bargain a few additional adjustments, in order to find the needed information on, say, *efficiō* s.v. *faciō.* What about compounds? *Frātricīda* is not listed separately, but is briefly alluded to under *frāter;* under *caedō* there is mention of the nominal segment *-cīda,* but with a different illustration. *Pāri-, parri-cīda,* on the other hand, figures separately, one gathers because the genetically elusive element *pār-/parr-* seems to have been attracted into the orbits of *pater* and *parēns* only through secondary rapprochement. Where the formal or the semantic relationship between primitive and derivative — or between important variants — has become loose, a helpful cross-reference is provided: s.vv. *coerceō* to *arceō, cōgitō* to *ag(it)ō, cognōmen* to *nōmen, colpus* to *colaphus, collūcō* to *lūcus, cōlō* to *cōlum,* and, with even greater justification on account of the margin of unpredictability involved, s.vv. *colurnus* to *corulus, combennōnēs* to *benne, combūrō* to *bustum* beside *ūrō, comminus* to *manus, commoetāculum* to *mūtō,* *compāgēs* to *pangō, conciēns* to *inciēns, condalium* to *condulus, cōnea* to *cicōnia, confarreātiō* to *far, conferua* to *ferrūmen,* etc. But where rare or esoteric variants are at issue, some of them sparingly or uniquely documented, the researcher is supposed to know on his own how to select for guidance the more common form of the word, and the network of cross-references is wholly omitted. Thus *conger* 'eel,' a Hellenism, is the only entry available; under it the curious reader will find mention of *congrus, gonger, gongrus/gungrus,* and [*] *grongus,* the last-mentioned pieced together from Romance dialectal reflexes. One stumbles over other rough spots. Thus, the triad *stō, sistō,* and **stanō* (as in *destinō*) has been consolidated into a single, complexly structured entry; so have the dyads *sīdō* and *sedeō, -cumbō* and *cubō,* while **-būrere,* for once, has not been pitted against *ūrere,* though it might have been extracted from *amb-ūrere* 'to scorch, singe' resegmented as *am-būrere,* judging from *bustum* 'pyre' and, above all, from *combūrere* 'to burn up, ruin.' Ernout, then, is very exacting toward his reader; what has been gained in concentration and clear vision ("Übersichtlichkeit") has been at the expense of easy, quick orientation conducive to relaxed reading.

Alphabetic arrangement, with some allowance for judicious tightening into lexical families, has, all told, become characteristic of a well-organized etymological dictionary, at least for a typical European language. Just what the conventional sequence of letters is in this context will in each instance depend on the circumstances. Gustav Meyer used for his dictionary of Albanian word origins (1891) this succession, within the general frame of the Latin alphabet: *a, b, d, δ, θ, e, f, g, ġ, h, x,* etc., a concatenation which is, clearly, inapplicable to other languages. Conversely, in lexical monographs either etymologically or, more broadly speaking, diachronically slanted, the consecutive alphabetic arrangement has proved unattractive, with two major exceptions. It has been preserved either (a) where the book is a mere companion volume to a straight etymological dictionary, a repository of additions and corrections, so to speak (as is true of N. Caix's *Studi di etimologia italiana e romanza* vis-à-vis F. Diez's *EWRS,* and of V. García de Diego's *Contribución* vis-à-vis the original edition of W. Meyer-Lübke's *REW*); or (b) where the book is a loose collection of randomly strung etymological notes, as is recognizable by, for instance, the absence of any forceful conclusion. An example in point is the Lund dissertation *Etymologische Studien zum Althochdeutschen* (1927) by Nils Otto Heinertz, which encompasses twenty unintegrated vignettes.

In most other cases the sequence of analyses will be presided over by referential considerations, either mathematical (in studies of numerals), or physical (in those of color names), or anatomico-physiological (cf. the inquiries into the designations of the parts of the human body and of their functions), or strictly social (cf. the investigations of kinship terms). One good example of the narrow-gauged lexical inquiry that has completely forsworn the alphabetic order (except, obviously, in the appended word indexes) is Maurice Cohen's study on one institutional facet of evanescent Nordic paganism, *Études sur le vocabulaire religieux du vieux-scandinave: la libation* (1921). The author constantly strives to maintain a precarious balance between "les faits de vocabulaire" (*Wörter*) and "les faits de civilisation" (*Sachen,* in the word's broadest sense); in his Introduction he emphatically declares himself primarily a linguist, as seems indeed to follow from the slightly superior elaborateness of his lexico-phraseological index (pp. 297-313) over his cultural index (pp. 315-22). But the discussions are arranged in a progression that seems to belie his claim: they range, thematically, from "Libation" through "The Festivals of Libation," the "Celebration of the Festivals," etc., all the way to the "Toast."

On a grand scale, one finds the culturally oriented structure adopted in Émile Benveniste's concluding masterpiece, *Le vocabulaire des institutions indo-européennes* (1969). Here the prime division is into the realms of economy, kinship, society, power, law, and religion. Benveniste had at his fingertips all the registers of linguistic (specifically, glottohistorical) research, and could have tilted or even bent his rich material at will in the direction either of straight linguistics or of cultural history. For once, he chose the latter course and, with admirable consistency, curbed the temptation of preparing a dictionary (invariably a kind of straitjacket) and chose instead the less-constrained genre of a lexical monograph.[1]

To return to the dictionaries, the Fick-Diez model has, on the whole, been abandoned, and only under very unusual circumstances does one run across more than a single succession of entries in a book, particularly one of post-1950 vintage. One such legitimate exception, in the subfield of paleo-Anatolian, is offered by E. Laroche's *Dictionnaire de la langue louvite.* Aside from the four appendages (in part grammatical, in part textual), the book contains, welded on to the main vocabulary (Luvian words transcribed, with Lycian and Hittite correspondences), also separate lists of "acephalous" words (pp. 116-18), of ideographs (pp. 119-25), and of proper names — including those of divinities and of localities (pp. 125-30). There exists too the type of overextended dictionary, with changes of design made in midstream, in response to new challenges and to new conditions of staffing. Thus, while W. von Wartburg's *FEW* for decades rolled off the press, fascicle after fascicle, as a highly elaborate, but unexceptionably well-ordered dictionary, the last years witnessed the segregation of all sorts of semiautonomous volumes within the swelling series, e.g., for Germanic bases and for Gallo-Romance words of wholly unidentifiable or irreducibly controversial parentage. Then again some etymologists cannot control their weakness for attaching to their dictionaries rather extended supplements, especially at the end of a concluding volume of a set; one example of this malpractice was supplied not so long ago by J. Corominas (see his *DCE,* IV, 897-1092). Finally, where two source languages are involved, however closely interwoven, it is at all times possible to advance arguments in favor of the listing of relevant words in two parallel series, in preference to interfiling. Thus, E. König segregated the Aramaic ingredients (pp. 561-606) from the bulk of the Hebrew words in his two-pronged Biblical dictionary, garnishing them with somewhat different etymological annotations.

Another bipartition, in a thesaurus of modern date (1956), is exhibited by A. Jóhannesson's *Isländisches etymologisches Wörterbuch.* The bulk of that book (pp. 1-933) is so arranged that the key entries are the roots culled from Walde-Pokorny's *VWIS* — collocated in an order which is at variance with that of our standard alphabet; namely in Latin script, but with numerous auxiliary phonetic symbols. To facilitate orientation for the uninitiated, these IE or Germanic bases have elsewhere (pp. 1233-44) been reshuffled so as to appear in strictly conventional and universally familiar alphabetic sequence. More important, all borrowings into Icelandic — principally, from Middle Low German, but also on a more modest scale from Celtic, Middle High German, Old French, and (Church) Latin — jointly form a separate major section (pp. 935-1231), which serves in addition — though this is nowhere prominently announced — as a shelter for isolated loan translations (such as *afskúm* after G. *Abschaum* 'scum') and for certain instances of folk etymology (as when *alpandyr* 'elephant' is traced to its Graeco-Latin origins via MLG *elpender,* but with a side-glance at native *dýr* 'animal' ~ G. *Tier,* E. *deer*). Finally, all Icelandic formations adduced can be located through a handy master list relegated to the very end (1245-1402), a list which is alphabetic, except that the sequence of letters allows for various idiosyncrasies of local usage —

with *ó* following upon *o*, *ý* following upon *y*, and *þ*, *æ*, *œ*, *ǫ*, *ϕ*, *ö*, and *ǭ* consigned to a position after *z*. Apart from frills, the first of the two major sections of Jóhannesson's dictionary is prospective and the second retrospective, yet, unlike V. García de Diego's experiment (1954), the two do not represent interdependent counterviews.

The use of different typographic symbols (superscript asterisks, square brackets) or fonts (bold face, small capitals) to discriminate between diverse categories of bases (reproduced with or without transliteration; transmitted by word of mouth or through books; recorded vs. reconstructed, etc.) serves an excellent purpose in certain contexts and amounts, in the last analysis, to an alternative to the Fick-Diez model of partitioning the entire corpus. In other contexts recourse to such qualifying devices would be supererogatory. R. Trautmann's *Baltisch-slavisches Wörterbuch* (1923), for instance, rests on the (controversial) assumption of a pristine Balto-Slavic "common stage." The entries are the bases reconstructed on that assumption – all of them, by definition, hypothetical. They are set off by spacing ("Sperrdruck") and need not be heralded by an asterisk – which the author, in turn, uses for Proto-Slavic (e.g., **ablъko* 'apple') and for Proto-Baltic (**ai-* or **ei-gūlā* 'needle'), in the absence of any other graphic emphasis.

The degree of selectivity can, by stretching the definition of grand strategy, also be subsumed under that dimension. Actually, very few etymological dictionaries aim at virtual exhaustiveness; Wartburg's *FEW* is one of the few exceptions that come to mind. But there is a difference between planned economy and desultory performance. P. F. Monlau's venture (1856, 1881) was a *Diccionario etimológico,* which provided comments, of varying merit and conviction, on all the important lexical items of the chosen language. R. Cabrera's posthumous *Diccionario de etimologías* (1837) was, in contrast, a noncommittal collection of stray identifications. A deep ravine – not just an interval of a few decades – separates these two experiments. In our own century, strings of etymological notes, such as Leo Spitzer's *Lexikalisches aus dem Katalanischen und den übrigen iberoromanischen Sprachen* (1921) – following in the wake of the same Romanist's shorter *Katalanische Etymologien* (1918) – would hardly qualify as a dictionary.

This does not mean, I repeat, that systematic reduction is of necessity detrimental to etymological research. Just as there exists in general the genre of abridged (short, pocket-sized, etc.) dictionaries –

witness F. Miklosich's *Dictionnaire abrégé des six langues slaves* (1885), comparatively but not genetically slanted — so there has developed the separate variety of a succinct, minimally argued and documented etymological dictionary, not infrequently a companion-piece to a more ambitious venture. The tell-tale qualifier "kurzgefaβt" appears in the titles of several well-thought-of Central European guides to etymology: M. Mayrhofer has chosen for his subtitle the English phrasing, *A Concise Etymological Sanskrit Dictionary* (1956-63), and J. Corominas' pleasingly lean *Breve diccionario* (1961, 1967), flanking his overextended and slightly verbose *DCE* (1954-57), clearly points in the same direction. In addition to such authorized extracts and epitomes, there have inevitably been some less welcome cases of dilution by uninvited popularizers, a few of whom have even been accused of gross plagiarism; one such controversial item was R. Plate's ill-fated etymological glossary of French.

One can think of several defensible criteria for compression. If etymological information is not the actual *raison d'être* of the book, then the words displayed as entries have, one hopes, been selected on some judicious basis (use by respected writers, acceptability to a prestigious group of speakers, and the like), and the availability or absence of a satisfactory etymology remains an incidental consideration. Recent editions of the Spanish Academy Dictionary are cases in point. Alternatively, such criteria as the commonness of the words as parts of a core vocabulary, or the transparency of their descent (or cogency of the etymological solutions offered) may be persuasively invoked.

6

THE STRUCTURE OF THE INDIVIDUAL ENTRY: TACTICAL PREFERENCES

The architectural design of the individual entry will depend on several circumstances, starting with the degree of centrality of the etymological message. If the etymological information is subsidiary or incidental, it will be capsulized in a brief parenthetic remark, which can best — i.e., least obtrusively — be accommodated either toward the very beginning or toward the end of the entry. The former possibility seems to enjoy a greater vogue. One finds it in the successive editions, since the late nineteenth century, of the Spanish Academy dictionary, also in Stratmann's Middle English Dictionary, brought up to date by H. Bradley. In each case the author and the reviser have laconically listed the Old English prototype, occasionally flanked by its Gothic cognate (s.v. *hēou* 'hue, color, species, form') − or, alternatively, the Middle Low German and Middle Dutch congeners (e.g., under *hepe* 'scythe'), and have then hurried on to the "descriptive" inventory of the entire paradigm, with as many extra-brief textual illustrations as possible marshaled for every single form. The identification is reduced to a concluding remark (sometimes of considerable length) in R. Menéndez Pidal's very elaborate − and, for its time (1908-11), masterly − *Cid* glossary.

Another preliminary condition is the degree of formality (achieved or aimed at) in organization and presentation. The eighteenth edition of Kluge's *EWDS,* revised by W. Mitzka, may be a jewel in terms of respectable popularization, but it cannot rank as a model of strictness. Certain entries begin with an anecdotal account of a relevant historical event or a custom (examples abound on every page; cf. s.vv. *Kandare, Kannibal, Kanton, Kanzel, Kanu, Kapaun, Kaplan*). Alongside this charming, if slightly chatty, approach, an alternative method used by the book involves a brief examination of the meaning, against the motley background of the word's record, with the sought-for etymological equation relegated to the very end (as happens s.v. *Kapotte*). In still another approach the reader is apprised of the word origin at the very start, and the justification is appended, as it were, to the key equation (s.vv. *Kapitel, kapores, Kapriole*). Such variety may offer a welcome relief and account for the extreme readability of "the Kluge," but is also redolent of a certain looseness or, perhaps, quaintness. Henceforth we shall be concerned with more formally arranged dictionaries.

The development toward enhanced formality has passed through several successive phases, which can be categorized when one studies subfields requiring a comparison between characteristic dictionaries, each pertaining to a different period. Thus, in Romance during the period of incubation, pioneering ventures such as those by Covarrubias and Ménage do contain a modicum of matter-of-fact information (especially on affixal derivatives); but much, indeed most, of the space is reserved for a loosely strung anecdotarium, each delightful story meant to re-create the historical moment which accounts for an otherwise inexplicable genetic link. By the middle of the nineteenth century, Diez's comparative dictionary marks a vigorous stride toward increased economy and stringency. Here, an entry is, predictably, ushered in by a concise inventory of relevant Romance cognates; there follows an exposition − not yet formulaic − of the favored hypothesis, or equally persuasive hypotheses, and a fairly prolix discussion of rival conjectures found lacking in cogency. Most of the available space is thus given over to a discursive − though very seldom polemic − treatment of the etymological puzzle.

The farther one advances, the more one finds the argumentative ingredient of etymology underplayed. S. Puşcariu's Rumanian dictionary (1905) contains all the paraphernalia of a technical twentieth-century reference work reserved for the expert: the listing of key words by numbers, the exploitation of contrastable fonts (including small capitals and boldface), the introduction of abbreviations, even for authors whose private epistolary communications are cited (P. for Papahagi) as well as for languages, key journals, and standard reference works, the sophisticated use of square brackets for Aromunian, Meglenitic, and Istro-Rumanian equivalents of different provenience, etc. The etymological discussion itself is, as a rule, brief, but there is no dearth of vignettes (s.vv. *mare* 'large' and *nepot* 'nephew,' say). The two versions of Meyer-Lübke's *REW* (1911-20, 1930-35) mark the next step. Here the preponderance of factual information over the analysis of competing explanations becomes even more pronounced; the rejection of ideas deemed infelicitous acquires a truly laconic twist (typical verdicts are: "scheitert an der Bedeutung," "formell unzulässig," and the like). The major novelty is the ingenious new system, already alluded to (see p. 5, above), for separating Romance innovations, esp. derivatives and compounds, from mere reverberations of the ancestral bases. The revised edition shows these features even more plastically, as fresh dialect data have been unstintingly included, whereas the addition of new explicative conjectures has been balanced by ruthless cutting out of deadwood.

W. von Wartburg's *FEW* − which began to appear midway through the time span which separates the two versions of Meyer-Lübke's *REW* − displays an even higher degree of formalization. A typical entry assumes the shape of a finely subdivided edifice of forms, with the conduit of transmission serving as the prime divider. The long parade of well-ordered reflexes leads up to a concluding, sparsely worded, essay-style analysis, which may run between ten and thirty lines and whose kernel is the sought-for etymon, often placed deftly and unobtrusively in its cultural context. Side issues, including those which bear on the authenticity of individual dialect forms and of gleanings from older texts and dictionaries, are tacitly relegated to notes assembled at the end of the given entry rather than at the bottom of each page, though they act as footnotes. The author pays the barest minimum of attention to the explicit refutation of alternative etymological solutions, and makes a point of consistently toning down any disagreements.

One recognizes, then, the emergence of an actual scale of gradual formalization, which runs parallel to increasing professionalism. While Covarrubias' dictionary was designed to instruct and entertain the curious and Diez's etymologicon appealed to a cultured élite rather than to a corps of specialists, Meyer-Lübke's and Wartburg's guides cannot be used profitably without careful preliminary training and thus belong in the hands of experts. If one accepts this scale as one yardstick for measuring progress, then it becomes patent that the *DCE* by J. Corominas, though published in the short span 1954-57, actually marks a retreat from the high water mark set by the *FEW*. Its outward resemblance to the latter in certain – essentially trivial – aspects, like monumentality, typographic tidiness, and use of footnotes, is heavily outweighed by such deep structural flaws as weakness of architectural design, lack of any sharp division between documentation and analysis, and, above all, an unhealthy dosage of polemic – not always doled out in dignified fashion, at that.

From our survey of progressive formalization it follows that the supporting scaffold of raw data plays a major rôle not only in the elucidation but also in the presentation of an etymology. Just as there exist, in general, dictionaries of widely varying sizes and measures of substance, so etymological dictionaries, as a subclass of lexicographic compilations, differ as to the mass of data operated on; again and again, the more elaborate ("thicker") venture not only boasts a wider range of uncommon words and a more generous supply of derivatives and compounds (the latter feature crucially important in German and ancient Greek), but also indulges in more elegant grouping of the material, as can be shown by comparing the modest etymological dictionary of Greek – produced in the afterglow of wartime conditions (1949) – by J. B. Hofmann with the higher-aiming *GEW* by Hjalmar Frisk (1960-72).[1]

THE STRUCTURE OF THE INDIVIDUAL ENTRY

Of more immediate relevance to the problem of the ideal structuring of the entry is the question: Just how many supporting data are actually needed to uphold a proposed etymological solution? One's first impulse is, perhaps, to declare: As many as possible. On second thought, the wisdom of a certain degree of economy or "leanness" becomes apparent, particularly after a quick glance at some over-extended dictionaries. Thus, a pioneer like B. P. Haşdeu was doubtless ill-advised in stuffing into the four fascicles of his *Etymologicum Magnum Romaniae* (1886-98) an almost unbelievable potpourri of — unquestionably serious — information: lengthy quotations from seventeenth-century sources, dialectological-folkloristic information about Daco-Rumanian (reports from Banat, Moldavia, Transylvania, . . .) and Macedo-Rumanian (with some folk songs quoted in full), synonymy, cognates in selected Balkan languages (especially Albanian), etc. The meager paragraph on the nucleus of the etymological problem is lost amid this flood of tangentially useful background information. On the other hand, where the centrality of the etymological message is not in jeopardy, a large quantity of extraneous information is, of course, unobjectionable. Thus, the deliberately brief etymological comment which forms a kind of incrustation for practically every second entry of A. Tobler and E. Lommatzsch's *AFW* is entirely appropriate, because the dictionary is not primarily etymological. In the perspective of 1975, Wartburg's ambitious *FEW* appears, in contrast, overextended, even though, unlike Haşdeu's *Etymologicum,* it fortunately did not expire at the BA- juncture. But the mass of patois and obsolescent dictionary forms paraded before the overwhelmed reader has a stifling effect in the end. To be sure, a thesaurus of Gallo-Romance dialects may, indirectly, feed an etymological dictionary, much as J. B. Hofmann's stewardship of the concordance-style *Thesaurus Linguae Latinae* stood him in excellent stead when he was called upon to revise A. Walde's highly concentrated *LEW.* But the *ThLL* and the *LEW*, nevertheless, remained separate projects, just as the Germanist consults the *Deutsches Wörterbuch* launched by J. and W. Grimm in 1852 and the explicitly etymological dictionary by Kluge as two mutually complementary, but always neatly distinguishable, "classics." In his frantic search for factual underpinning, Wartburg — thus revealing himself to be an early-twentieth-century alumnus of Zürich University — appears to have overreached himself.

Apart from the issue of optimal quantities, there is also that of the quality of corroborative material. Here several questions arise for which it is difficult to find a common denominator. Is the compiler of an etymological dictionary responsible for the accuracy of all data? Can he be expected to short-circuit faulty editions of ancient and medieval texts and go directly back to the manuscripts and inscriptions? What about the check on dialect data, which, even under the most favorable circumstances, can, if executed of late, neither prove nor disprove the correctness of a record made half a century ago? Should the different systems of phonetic transcription used by various schools of field workers and by a few maverick explorers be left intact, or should one standard system be ruthlessly imposed on all data? What about the transliteration of the data adduced — should everything in a comparative Slavic dictionary appear in Latin script, or should Latin, Glagolitic, and Cyrillic be used on a par, to say nothing of the multifariousness of scripts theoretically available to a comparative Semitologist? How far, in other words, should interpretation be allowed to go, and to what extent is it advisable to strive toward homogeneity as a preliminary to all-important comparability?

The answers will vary from case to case. An expert of Ernout's rank is certainly expected to offer emendations — in other words, to act simultaneously as textual critic and etymological analyst. Lommatzsch, an accomplished medievalist, made a point of distilling the entire collection of Old French material before making it accessible and testing against it the espoused etymological conjecture. Wartburg double- and triple-checked each form cited (and later did a splendid job of proofreading), but avoided any imposition of uniformity on the diverse data, some of them retrieved from muddy waters.

The single most successful thrust in the direction of homogeneity could conceivably be undertaken by an etymologically inspired student of dialects who could be persuaded to prepare an index of the genetic clues to all regional words collected, through interviews or tape recordings, in the course of a single major atlas project. Thus Karl Jaberg scrupulously prepared an Italian Index and a parallel Raeto-Romance Index (both mainly descriptive) to the *AIS* — published posthumously, in 1960. Since all the words were elicited and transcribed under comparable if not strictly identical conditions, a future etymological companion volume, if ever undertaken, would involve impeccably homogeneous material.

As a matter of fact, even in its present state, Jaberg's *Index* — as its subtitle and a core section of the substantial Introduction both manifest — represents an etymological vocabulary *sui generis*, which the compiler was perhaps ill-advised to dub — unconventionally — "propaedeutical." Through a simple typographic device (the contrasting of lower-case roman with small capitals), the *Index* sets off key words ("Stichwörter") from the mass of regionalisms drifting through Italian and Western Raeto-Romance dialect speech; these heedfully selected key words are either the representatives of a given lexical family in Standard Italian (and thus readily ascertainable in etymological literature) or — and it is in this alternative that Jaberg's flair for word origins and analytical acumen are brought into play — they are the dialect forms closest in form and meaning to the presumed etymon. This last consideration vindicates the labeling of the dictionary as etymological in a "preliminary" or "introductory" — better still, "initiatory" — sense.[2]

Attention has already been drawn, apropos of Ernout and Meillet's *DÉLL* and H. Frisk's *GEW*, to certain benefits attaching to the joint genetic consideration of entire lexical families rather than the frittering away of one's energy and intuition on individual unintegrated words. The higher degree of abstraction implicit in the bolder synopsis carries with it both richer rewards and heavier risks, a few of which have still to be identified.

The chief advantage is the closer meshing of lexicon and grammar, particularly the latter's morphological ingredient — above all, affixal derivation, on which lexicon and grammar have long been known to abut.

Undeniably, the student of morphology can winnow out of a routinely arranged etymological dictionary a wealth of valuable information on various classes and combinations of affixes, on multifarious compositional designs, and the like. A major economy is achieved if the etymologist at work on a many-faceted entry, instead of lumping together a congeries of data and hypotheses into a single amorphous paragraph, agrees to separate and, by so doing, to preanalyze the grammatical and the cultural nuggets of information — equally yet diversely relevant.

Thus, to cite one example at random, Ernout and Meillet manage to organize two discrete — but subtly interconnected — entries: *satis* 'enough, much' and *satur* 'stuffed full, surfeited.' *Satis,* for them, merits attention first as an adverb, through analysis of its constructions; second, as a member of certain verbal juxtapositions (*satisfaciō* 'I satisfy'); third, in truncated form, as the radical segment of a few characteristic derivatives, including the abstract *satietās* and the verb

47

satiō. Under *satur*, the adjectival primitive is, in turn, set off from nominalized *sat-ira/-ura* 'dish of mixed fruits,' fig. 'farce' and from such primary offshoots — once removed from the primitive — as the adverbial abstract *saturitās* and the verb *saturō*, beside which the authors place a sprinkling of secondary offshoots, chiefly the verbal abstracts *satur-ātiō* and *-āmen*. Only then, after Meillet's projection of the etymological problem onto the IE plane, does the reader learn from a triptych of additional entries that neither *satureia*$_1$ (sg.) = *cunila* 'savory,' nor *satureia*$_2$ (pl.) 'a certain aphrodisiac herb' — provided it is at all defensible to discriminate between these two phytonyms — nor indeed *Sāturnus,* the familiar name of an Italic divinity (of Etruscan provenience?), is genetically related to the family at issue, or, for that matter, to either of the other two. Thus, several categories of scholars — students of syntax (via *satis*), those of suffixation and juxtaposition (via *satis-, sati-*, etc.), those of material civilization, the arts, and mythology (via *satura, Sāturnus*) — have, through a single stroke of master strategy, been enabled to encounter immediately the shreds of specific information they are eager to detect. At the same time, there has emerged, to the satisfaction of the semanticist, a multi-layered lexical picture of 'surfeit.' Meanwhile, the paleo-Indo-Europeanist is rewarded here and there with a smooth introduction to certain vocalic variants of the stem, cf. the authors' pithy comment on *scobis* 'filings, chips' under *scabō* 'to scratch', and many similar remarks.

The use of a dictionary which subordinates individual words to families of varying size would be a source of unadulterated pleasure were it not for the fact that this arrangement produces new difficulties for the geneticist — not only organizational ones — beyond those peculiar to the familiar intricate "case histories." The discrepancies between rival analyses, far from diminishing, are apt to increase in number and, above all, in size, as can be dramatized by a comparison of two equally modern and inherently excellent etymological distillations of the Latin vocabulary, one by Ernout and Meillet (*DÉLL*), the other by Hofmann as a reviser of Walde (*LEW*). Here are a few illustrations of the new crop of problems.

The *LEW* assigns separate niches to *sigillum* 'small figure' and *sīgnum* 'sign, mark, token'; the *DÉLL* subsumes them under a single entry and, in the process, opts for the var. *signum,* with ĭ, appealing to the testimony of Romance (It. *segno,* [Sp. *señas* and *señal*]). The *LEW* separates *similis* 'similar' from *simulācrum* 'image, likeness, portrait, effigy,' paying considerable attention to the suffix *-ācrum,* which it places alongside the final segment of *mīrāculum* 'wonder' and *spectāculum* 'sight, show' (except for the effects of syncope and of the dissimilation of sonorants); the *DÉLL* brackets *simulācrum* with *similis,* disregarding any and all phonetic and derivational complications and focusing attention instead on (a) the word's palette of meanings, (b) its relation to Gr. *eídōlon,* and (c) its polarization against *rēs* and *corpus.* The *LEW* examines jointly the triad *dēstinō* 'to make fast, fix, settle,' *obstinō* 'to persist,' and (Plautus) *praestinō* 'to fix in advance the price, buy,' but refuses to go any further into levels of abstraction and subsumption. Its competitor operates with **stanō* (without being able to pin down the meaning of the reconstruction) and links it to the far-flung empire of *stō* 'to stand' and reduplicative-causative *sistō* 'to set, place, stop, check' (lit. 'to cause to stand still'). The *LEW* endorses the joint treatment of *stō* and *sistō* and throws in, for good measure, the suffix of *agre-stis* 'belonging to the field, rustic, bovine' and *cael-estis* 'heavenly,' an association at which the *DÉLL,* for once, balks, seeing in *-stis* a mere variant of *-stris,* as in *camp-estris* '[lying] flat, on level ground,' *silv-estris* 'wooded, wild,' and *terr-estris* 'pertaining to the earth.' Walde and Hofmann go no farther than to throw bridges from *cōnsīderō* 'to regard carefully, reflect upon' to *dēsīderō* 'to long for, miss, find a lack of' and to *praesīderō* 'to start early' (in reference to the winter); they allow for no formal cross-reference to *sīdus -eris* 'star,' even though they support this etymology, traceable to Antiquity (Paulus ex Festo), indeed buttress it with a suggestive parallel (*contemplor* 'to look at attentively,' from *templum* 'consecrated ground, sanctuary, shrine'), evoking specific channels of transmission: "Wohl urspr[ünglich] ein t[erminus] t[echnicus] der Seemannssprache oder ev[entuell] der Auguralsprache: 'die Sterne beobachten bzw. mit dem Blick zusammenfassen.' " Ernout and Meillet provide a similar analysis: "... d'anciens termes de la langue augurale ... laïcisés en passant dans la langue courante," but, unlike their German counterparts, draw a tactical conclusion from this incontrovertible fact and accommodate the three verbs under the vastly expanded entry *sīdus -eris.* On the whole, then, the Parisian dictionary is operationally bolder than its Munich rival — which, after all, goes back to a distinctly older prototype (the dates for Walde's *LEW* are 1906 and 1910). Still, the magnitude of discrepancy between two oft-invoked authorities remains a source of amazement and frustration.

The arrangement of languages tapped and cited, particularly in dictionaries prospectively exhibiting the relationships, can be made in a variety of ways — the simplest but least enlightening being the array of the various "daughter languages" in their alphabetical order. More sophisticated (and, one suspects, more common at this advanced stage of organized research) is the geographic grouping, especially if it can be combined with a modicum of genetic refinement through operation with subfamilies or, at least, through sustained attention to close affinities and alliances — as a result of whatever circumstances — between certain members of a far-flung family. Burrow and Emeneau have taken one important step in this direction. The implied entries in their *DED* are phonemically reconstructed proto-Dravidian bases; these are withheld from the casual reader, who is offered instead, immediately after an identification number, a string of reflexes laid out in, essentially, geographic progression — from south to north — but with certain mild concessions to the genetic principle of ordering, as explained in the Introduction (p. xxi). Thus Tamil and Malayalam go together, on the one hand, and Kolami, Naiki, Parji, and Gadba, on the other; the user is left free to subsume Gondi and Koṇḍa as well as Kui and Kuwa under two small subfamilies (for which no labels are supplied) or, alternatively, to view all four as diverging members of a single large subfamily; and he is forewarned that, according to the latest thinking, Toda should not have been wedged in between Kota and Kannaḍa, but quite justifiably grouped with Tamil and Malayalam, while its kinship to Kota remains problematic. It is interesting that the treatment of Tamil as the "favorite daughter" is due not only to geographico-genetic considerations, but also to the availability, since 1939, of a particularly copious *Tamil Lexicon* in six volumes (which often furnishes the semantic leads "needed to rationalize the inclusion of seemingly dissimilar items within the same group") and to the fact that the alphabet pressed into service in recording and ordering all prototypes has been the Tamil alphabet (p. xx); conceivably the high number of speakers of Tamil and its prestige as one of the four literary languages within the family have been reinforcing factors. Thus, the authors' decisions represent a compromise between the dictates of science and those of practicality and, in this respect, resemble the canons to which K. Jaberg, stationed in a different part of the world, adhered independently during those same years.

Whereas, in a tightly structured comparative dictionary, it was normal, as late as the time of Berneker, to have each language represented by only one carefully selected form, the irrepressible yearning for improvement and elaboration has prompted scholars to resort to ever more delicate nuancing. The forms adduced from attested languages to justify an etymological equation can be legitimately qualified in a variety of ways — through specification of (a) the locale (regional dialect or subdialect), (b) the source of attestation (literary text, gloss or dictionary entry, inscription, field note), (c) the date, exact or approximate, and (d) the register (in sociolinguistic terms) or the stylistic level — in short, (α) the occasion for the utterance or written use and (β) the environment, i.e., the socioeducational status of the expected hearers or readers.[3] To this network may be added, as the fifth qualification (e), the authenticity of the records — since spurious philological readings and hasty, inaccurate field notes have at all times been sources of phantom words, notoriously difficult to weed out once they have struck root in respected reference works.

Examples of the increasing use of all five techniques of refinement can be provided in almost unlimited numbers:

(a) Whereas Diez, in his *EWRS*, utilized dialect sources very sparingly — for Gallo-Romance (say), the only more or less dependable dictionary of that kind available to him at the mid-century point was Volume I (1845) of Charles Grandgagnage's *Dictionnaire étymologique de la langue wallonne* — one observes an overflow of such sources in Meyer-Lübke's *REW* and an inundation in Wartburg's *FEW*. Under such circumstances, all kinds of sigla — some of them, perhaps unavoidably, puzzling — have to be introduced, and the reading of an average article threatens to become an exacting task, especially onerous if inconsistencies in abbreviations have been allowed to slip in. Thus, Meyer-Lübke, upon his own admission, used "alb." for 'the Piedmontese dialect of Albi,' but also — alongside "alban." — for 'Albanian'; either "ard." or "ardenn.," prefixed to a form, referred in his dictionary to 'the patois of Ardennes'; either "berr." or "berrich." (in tribute to the derivative "Berrichon") signaled 'Berry'; "Haute-Auvergne" was hardly an elegant match for "Hochnavarra"; and tiny hamlets, invisible on an ordinary map but sometimes investigated in depth, like Cespedosa de Tormes (whose speech, half a century ago, yielded a fine specimen of Eastern Leonese), were placed hierarchically on the same plateau as major provinces, bearing names familiar to everyone.

Despite certain abuses and shortcomings, accurate localization is, needless to say, more than welcome and serves many useful purposes. In the case of presumed borrowings through slow infiltration (rather than through "parachuting"), the habitat of the given words functions as a prime clue to their ancestry. Thus, the fact that *kantham* 'town' is restricted to toponyms in northwest India enables M. Mayrhofer to trace it with considerable plausibility to its Iranian source.

(b) All self-respecting lexicographers set aside words transmitted only through glosses. As regards the initiative of individual writers (sometimes hidden behind anonymous texts), a relatively small, but compactly organized guide, such as Dubois and Mitterand's skillful revision (1964: *NDÉH*) of Dauzat's *DÉLF* — a book which, in line with its sponsorship by the aggressive Larousse firm, is bound to appeal to a vast, literate, broadly curious, and esthetically oriented readership — somehow succeeds in conveying a modicum of quintessential information on this point under the majority of entries. Thus, to pick out one example from among thousands, the *NDÉH* not only credits the tentative launching of *investigation* to Christine de Pizan, but also singles out Rousseau as the master of French prose who, centuries later, revitalized the word after a period of slackening. The particular source of strength from this refurbished French dictionary is doubtless due to the newly concluded or briskly advancing lexical "dépouillements" by B. Quemada, P. Robert, and other researchers similarly inspired (see Introduction, p. v).

(c) There is widespread consensus on the wisdom of this feature, and progress has been universal. In this respect, it is instructive to compare the chronological reticence of a W. W. Skeat in his *Concise Etymological Dictionary* (originally published, to be sure, over ninety years ago, but thoroughly revised in 1901, even more so by 1911) with the modern explicitness of the Oxford volume produced by the Onions team — though satisfied, as a rule, with merely stating the century. And yet, one can visualize prospects of further improvement on a grandiose scale — through much closer attention to the ailing, submergence, and irreversible extinction of words; to the time during which they oozed from one stratum of the lexicon to another (as when a word long-confined to technical use — like *ecology, euphoria, phonetics, plethora, semantics* — all at once becomes common, or a heretofore colorless, inconspicuous, and occasionally specialized word, such as Russ. *sputnik,* lit. 'companion,' fig. 'satellite,' rises to prominence, as a result of a scientific breakthrough, and suddenly becomes subject to diffusion); and to repeated or multiple coinage or borrowing, each sponsor being, typically, unaware of having had one or more predecessors. One could thus plot the temporal record of a word as a combination of dotted lines, straight lines, and curves, perhaps interspersed with blanks — just as a lexical item's geographic spread (cf. Point [a], above) may be dramatized by a miniature map. The oft-revised Bloch-Wartburg dictionary (*DÉLF*) has been particularly attentive to consecutive (independent) introductions of the same word.[4]

(d) The social register or stylistic level may be — philologically — implied in the source: Pompeii graffiti are scurrilous, Plautine plays offer specimens of racy colloquial Latin while those by Terence exemplify polished conversational discourse, Vergil attains the ultimate in refinement in all his writings, Ovid may be perverse or obscene but refuses to stoop to crudeness, St. Jerome's Bible translation is more elegant than the Vetus Latina (or Itala), and Prudentius — as a deliberately archaizing poet — aims to emulate Augustan models rather than reflecting the "eroded" speech of his own century and immediate environment. Authors of the better etymological dictionaries rightly expect their "customers" to carry such elementary knowledge into their reading and consulting: the parenthetic mention of a writer's name will suffice if his works show little lexico-stylistic heterogeneity. On the other hand, Cicero's speeches reek with rhetoric, while his more intimate letters contain none; Horace used two different keys as a satirist and as a composer of odes; Pushkin's prose and poetry are geared to entirely different selections of words; Goethe, as a result of his longevity and resilience, used in his juvenilia a German at variance with the language he cultivated as an old man. In such contexts the etymologist will be well-advised to supply, in his corroborative comment, the writer's name and the title of the work.

The situation is different again where field notes are, at least in part, involved. Thus, the compilers of the *DED* have relied chiefly on written sources for Tamil, Kannaḍa, Malayalam, and Telugu, but have fallen back on Emeneau's still unpublished field notes for Kota, Toda, and Koḍagu (at rare intervals also for Badaga), and on Burrow's and Bhattadrarya's for Naiki and Adilabad Gondi (*inter alia*) — because printed material was either nonexistent or, as seems to be the case with Gondi, "deplorable" (Introduction, pp. xviii-xix). Under such restricting circumstances, contextual hints and eye-witness remarks are possible, though the compilers of the *DED* seem to have decided on a course of parsimoniousness in supplying any (cf., under 2007, Go. *sāhatāna* 'to stretch out [one's hands or feet, as women do when fighting]'). The penciling in of the participants' mood, typical moment or season, social conditions, etc., attendant upon an event capsulized rather than captured in a brief lexical entry depends, naturally, on the training, personal taste, and scholarly intentions of the explorer.

(e) The references qualifying the authenticity of certain components of the record will vary with the degree of philological scrupulosity of each etymologist. Often a question mark will serve to voice surprise or skepticism, or to impose caution. Burrow and Emeneau sometimes use one before a cited form or before the prefixed abbreviation for a language, to adumbrate the direction of their doubt. The original division of labor on the *DÉLL* between Ernout and Meillet relieved the former of all responsibility for the IE prelude (outside Italic), allowing him to concentrate his attention on a uniquely meticulous filtering of the material garnered. Mayrhofer neatly distinguishes, again and again, between items actually extracted from literature, hence observable in context, and others, apparently of a lower degree of credibility, known solely from listings in dictionaries ("unbelegt," "Lexikonwort": e.g., *kaccaraḥ, kaṭaḥ, kaṭāḥaḥ₃*).

The actual *raison d'être* of etymology and, consequently, the inner sanctum of an etymological dictionary is, of course, the edifice of elucidations of word origins. There exist several characteristic and recurrent styles for presenting the sought-for solutions; to some extent, these styles co-vary with the formats of the given dictionaries, since it might be paradoxical to indulge in lengthy explanations where the size available for the whole book is so limited as to impose austerity.

If one agrees to disregard, for a while, all manner of transitions, the basic possibilities seem to be these: the etymologist either (a) dryly lists the source word under the given entry (unless he flatly states that the origin is unknown); (b) supplies the etymon, with a split-second glimpse of the surrounding cultural scene or a succinct glottohistorical comment; (c) champions the most likely solution, but remains aware of alternative possibilities and attempts to rank such etyma in the − descending or ascending − order of their plausibility; (d) views one solution as entirely, or almost entirely, satisfactory, and the rest, which he also makes a point of mentioning, as wholly misleading, frequently engaging in the explicit refutation of the heresies; (e) identifies overtly just one solution, and ordinarily by so doing underwrites it, but supplies a sufficient quota of "assorted literature" to enable the better-qualified among his readers to venture on their own into the thicket of pending controversies; or (f) provides particulars – with full bibliographic details and allusive assessments – on the preceding discussion, either randomly or by selecting one of the two available standard techniques for formal presentation of the given "historique du problème" – in addition to advocating one favorite hypothesis (either of his own making or selected from among those previously proffered). There exist all sorts of significant and sometimes imaginative variations. A scholar may attempt to revive a conjecture long regarded as antiquated and worthless, by shoring it up with new arguments; or he may, with one bold stroke, strive to raise a word's source long held to be secondary to the higher status of a primary source, etc. Occasionally the rehabilitation of older authorities will be accompanied by an analysis of the fallacy that prompted a later generation or school of thought (e.g., the Neogrammarians) to discredit them.

In most of these situations, the seasoned etymologist will be tempted to nuance his reactions to a long list of probabilistic statements: his own hypotheses, those that he adopts from others (not without at least slight modifications as a rule), and, above all, those that he impugns. A stylistically versatile author of an etymological dictionary need not confine himself to wholehearted acceptance of certain conjectures nor to morose condemnation of others. He is free to couch his verdicts – through use of lexical and syntactic devices, and even by cleverly manipulating question and exclamation marks (permitted in the tradition of German scholarship) – in such a way as to convey the precise modulations of his voice. Thus, Mayrhofer's Sanskrit dictionary abounds in opulently orchestrated responses to challenges from many quarters; the author goes far beyond stating that a predecessor's judgment seems to him convincing, likely, entirely possible, just barely conceivable, or utterly unrealistic.[5]

To revert to our scheme of six basic classes of etymological proposals – here are a few concrete illustrations of each.

(a) The type of etymological vocabulary or compendium that aims at bare identification of word origins – without even the redeeming comparative component – became conspicuously rare, particularly in Europe,[6] after the First World War. Such restraint was, for a while, observable in glossaries, including a few by top-notch specialists, if the etymological information represented a mere sideline of the total commitment. In W. Foerster's exhaustive Chrétien glossary (orig. ed. 1914), this sparseness reached its peak; but the book made up for it mainly through the wealth of the inventory of forms (including those of troublesome verbs) and through accurate localization of each passage, to say nothing of the value of the compiler's introductory remarks (pp. 210*-223*) on the poet's language, as reconstructed from the idiosyncrasies of scribes, the whole against the backdrop of Foerster's general reputation as diachronicist (witness his celebrated paper on Romance metaphony) and of his unique familiarity with Chrétien. Even more eloquent is the example of C. Michaëlis de Vasconcelos' glossary to the *Cancioneiro da Ajuda,* published in the early twenties but actually compiled ca. 1905. A superb practitioner of discursively styled etymology "for its own sake" in other contexts,[7] she imposed upon herself utmost austerity and parsimoniousness for a change.[8]

Again, H. Tiktin's chief purpose in compiling his long-authoritative *Rumänisch-deutsches Wörterbuch* (3 vols., 1903-25), a fairly typical bilingual dictionary, was to avoid diverting the user's attention through an unwelcome incrustation of etymological speculations. So, as a rule he stated the word origin with commendable brevity toward the end of each entry (e.g., s.vv. *braţară, brătaş, braţeta, brazdă, bre!, brehăi, bricin*) or candidly admitted ignorance along that axis (s.vv. *breben-e* and *-e-c, brehnace, brighidău, brîglă, brilioncă, brînduşă, briolă*), specifying the area of his doubt (s.v. *brătucă*) or engaging only occasionally in discursive analysis (s.vv. *breslă, brez, briceg, brînză*). But behind his laconisms stood at all times the prestige he had earned by contributing a weighty encyclopedia-style chapter to Gröber's *Grundriß* and, above all, by writing his sophisticated historical grammar titled, almost ironically, *Rumänisches Elementarbuch* (1905).

A less forgivable instance of explicative economy, bordering on aridity, is offered by F. Holthausen's *Altenglisches etymologisches Wörterbuch,* which one might have expected to be more meaty. The beginning of an average entry, in which the author strives to surround the chosen Anglo-Saxon word with a host of Germanic congeners, is promising enough; but once this quick parade is over, the reader is presented with a bare identification of the base and is, more often than not, anticlimactically referred for further details to Walde-Pokorny's IE dictionary. One comes away with the painful impression that the task of writing this particular dictionary — one of several undertaken by Holthausen — was a source of boredom to the author: Instead of kaleidoscopically re-creating, via the lexicon, sundry elements of the oldest tangible slices of English culture, he humbly did yeoman's service for the Indo-Europeanist.

As we approach more complex and intricate forms of etymological pronouncements, it becomes clear that the matter of equilibrium between the onset or forematter of an entry and the kernel of the etymological analysis has been on the minds of many scholars. Victor Henry, for one, arranged his *Lexique étymologique des termes les plus usuels du breton moderne* in such a way that the Celtic cognates of the key word form the opening part of each article, preceding the identifiction of the etymon, whereas the remote IE congeners cluster around the base, signifying pertinence to the concluding part. Thus, apropos of the preposition *war* 'on' the reader is first introduced to M. Br. *(v)oar,* Corn. *gur > war,* Cymr. *guar/guor > gor* . . .; then, after becoming sensitized to the existence of the source word [Proto-] Celt. **wer < *u(p)er,* he is treated to a network of relations, e.g., Sanskr. *upári,* Gr. ὑπέρ, Lat. *super,* etc. In other cases (e.g., s.v. *warléné* [adv.] 'last year,' originally a compound), the etymological dissection is even more heavily weighted than the preliminary marshaling of cognates.

Aside from the purely esthetic preoccupation with symmetry, there is also a necessity for the analyst to make certain choices within a more or less fixed budget of time, printing expenses, and competing investments. If N. Å. Nielsen's admirably condensed *Dansk Etymologisk Ordbog* provides a modicum of clues to technical literature and cites exuberant quantities of cognates, its author cannot be expected, in all fairness, to stuff the book — already brimful — with copious references to older texts or to engage in profuse advocacy of the etymon endorsed. Etymological dictionaries of French aiming at the domestic market (Dauzat's *DÉLF,* say) have a right to pay closer attention to the local record of each word (rough date of appearance, channels, semantic curve; see above) than to certain prosodic niceties in the structure of its prototype or to the entry's affinity to some congener in far-off Numidia, Dalmatia, or Sardinia. Also, the character of the book or series as a whole may mould the configuration of an entry.[9] With these qualifications in mind, let us revert to the classes (b) through (f) of etymological commitments, as previously posited.

(b) The etymological solution can be made more interesting and more readily assimilable through a brief accompanying comment. While there are presumably as many different styles and slants available for such remarks as there are authors, certain unifying tendencies stand out quite sharply. As a rule, the comment leans in the direction either of phonology and morpho-syntax or of the cultural ambiance assumed to have surrounded the word's genesis as well as the early — mostly hidden — stages of its growth and migrations. The choice of either emphasis hinges on an interplay of two factors: (α) the contrast between the Indo-Europeanist tradition, on the one hand, preponderantly abstract in the absence of direct access to the parent language, hence prone to stress grammatical matters (*lato sensu*), and the Romanist tradition (or its analogues), on the other, operating with a very thoroughly explored parent language projected against a familiar segment of world history, hence culture-oriented; and (β) the chosen or anticipated level of readership, given the fact that the appeal of comparative grammar to the best-intentioned lay reader never matches his engrossment with cultural history. Hence the immense — and richly deserved — popularity, within the community of "modern-language experts," of Bloch-Wartburg's *DÉLF*, which intersperses austere equations with spicy nuggets of cultural information in just the right proportion, in contrast to the strictly grammatical and comparatist bias of, say, F. Tamm's *Etymologisk Svensk Ordbok* — a classic of stern Scandinavian workmanship (which, unfortunately, did not progress beyond the torso stage). One would assume that intense concern with shades of meaning is ordinarily accompanied by broad cultural rather than narrow grammatical curiosity, but there are exceptions from this pattern of affinity. Thus, J. Jakobsen's Shetlandic dictionary, in its microscopic survey of data, is exceptionally elaborate on the side of semantic hues (and of the phonetic variants — many of them collected in the field throughout a lifetime of unremitting enthusiasm). Conversely, it is rather economical with comments on the cultural background — restricted, it would seem, to contexts in which the author has to hand down a difficult etymological decision.

(c) The mention of several etymological possibilities — often left unhierarchized as to degree of verisimilitude — was characteristic of the older style of inquiry (S. de Covarrubias, G. Ménage) and later led science historians to speculate that the pioneers frequently had unpublished lists of rival conjectures before them, between which they found it painful to make appropriate choices. In modern scholarship inferior solutions are tacitly omitted as a rule from "concise etymological dictionaries" or from incidental etymological comments wedged into standard dictionaries. There also exist ways and means to curtail their importance or, if need be, to tone them down in more formal contexts through an allusive rather than explicit approach. Thus, H. H. Bender, in his *Lithuanian Etymological Index* (1921), adopted the following technique: after going through the ritual of documenting the Lithuanian word at issue in certain standard works devoted principally to cognate languages (Boisacq, Feist, Walde, etc.), he started the second half of each entry with the abbreviation "cf." — used divisively rather than connectively — and then set out to glean further genetic references to the word, made by less frequently invoked authorities, using round parentheses to indicate discrepant interpretations and square brackets to indicate oblique, rather than direct, endorsements. Thus any alternative solution is barely hinted at, though the reader obtains a discreet clue to the locus and can satisfy his curiosity, if it has been sufficiently aroused.

In certain areas of linguistic knowledge (e.g., the domains of Greek, Latin, and Romance) a plurality of etymologies suggested over the years can almost be taken for granted; in other provinces this appears to be exceedingly rare. Thus, a scholar as well-versed in Indics as Ralph L. Turner offered very copious arrays of cognates in his *Comparative and Etymological Dictionary of the Nepali Language* (1931), as could be expected of an expert gradually working, or groping his way, toward his ambitious synthesis, *A Comparative Dictionary of Indo-Aryan Languages* (1966); but he included surprisingly few and astonishingly meager etymological discussions — just here and there a conciliatory hint of bolder connections posited by one of a handful of specialists — a Jules Bloch (*La formation de la langue marathe*, 1915); a W. Geiger (*Etymologie des Singhalesischen*, 1898); a G. A. Grierson (*The Piśāca Language in Northwestern India*, 1906); or a G. Morgenstierne (*An Etymological Dictionary of Pashto*, 1927, and *Indo-Iranian Frontier Languages*, 1929-67). If one compares this record of acquiescence with the stridency of certain Romance etymologists, one becomes curious about the circumstance which accounts for the contrast: Is the corpus of technical literature on Indo-Aryan still so small that it has not yet given rise to controversies worthy of attention? Is the lexicon of the Nepali language genetically so diaphanous — despite its Tibeto-Burmese substratum, recognized by Turner — as to leave fewer evolutionary uncertainties than the vocabulary of a typical Western language? Or does the tradition of research in this "esoteric" domain demand a chivalrous playing-down of even honest differences of opinion?

(d) The espousal of one solution in preference to certain others, specifically identified and credited to their respective advocates, then explicitly rejected, is characteristic of fields boasting an extensive body of sharply profiled etymological literature. One intriguing borderline case is provided by a candid admission of ignorance, pitted against a surrender to a facile, only partially convincing, hypothesis. Thus, forty years ago a perplexed Meyer-Lübke, in the definitive version of his Romance dictionary, had the courage to confess his inability to pin down the provenience of [*] *tīrāre* (8755: "Woher? — Ursprung unbekannt"). In the process he repudiated, among the respectable if less than cogent conjectures known to him, (i) Goth. *taíran* 'to tear' as phonologically inadequate (in fact, as being no less vulnerable than its semantic counterpart Fr. *déchirer* in the latter's relation to its assumed Frankish prototype); both (ii) Frk. *tir* 'fame' (G. Cohn) and (iii) the blend *taíran* × Gr.-Lat. *gȳrāre* 'to turn' (E. Gamillscheg, *EWFS₁*) as semantically unsatisfactory, and (iv) Ch. L. (< Gr.) **martyrāre* (Serra) 'to torture a witness for the faith by rending his body' as being morphologically startling — the disappearance of a first syllable, unless it happens to be a prefix that can be sloughed off, is indeed bizarre. After Meyer-Lübke's abdication of the authority vested in him the disposal of waste and debris was expeditiously concluded: Friul. *tirulis* 'robust' and Fr. *attirail* 'embellishment' (cf. OFr. *atirier* 'to prepare') were moved out of the way and assigned to other families, which offered niches more suitable for them.

Not surprisingly, Gamillscheg, in redesigning the entry for his own revised dictionary (*EWFS₂*) thirty-five years later, reached entirely different conclusions. Though aware of the facts and considerations that Meyer-Lübke had adduced and of others that his teacher had swept under the rug — e.g., of a codicil to Serra's conjecture (**mar-* > **mal-tirare*) — and though mindful of later accretions to the stock of hypotheses (e.g., Wartburg's appeal to *mar-* < *malā hōrā* as the medieval prefix of 'jinx', and E. Lerch's reliance on the concomitant influence of *tirant* 'tyrant'), Gamillscheg still felt that an amalgam of *taíran* (from Gmc. *tëran*) and *gȳrāre* promised the smoothest solution.

The core of his critique is worth pondering:

> . . . schon deshalb unmöglich, weil **tirare* aus einer zu allen Zeiten lebendigen Wortfamilie herausgeschnitten würde, ohne in eine begriffsverwandte schon vorhandene Wortfamilie eingereiht zu werden, und weil *tirare* 'ziehen' kein 'martern, quälen' ist.

Thus, even though the two scholars — teacher and star pupil —

infer radically divergent conclusions from virtually the same set of circumstances, their style of presentation remains the same, details aside.

The technique applied by Vasmer falls into a class by itself. Although his dictionary ostensibly deals with Russian, two entries out of every three come closer to fitting the needs of comparative Slavic research (in the tradition of Miklosich and Berneker), with constant attention to the entire IE domain by way of background. As a consequence, most of the space is allotted to rapprochements, first with the closer and, on a second tier, with the more distant ("urverwandt") cognates. The apparatus attached is short (in comparison with the "Sekundär-literatur" adduced by Meyer-Lübke or Walde and Hofmann) and, in the overwhelming majority of articles, lacks any critical, let alone polemic, overtones (cf. s.vv. *drápat'*, *dróžži*). The most dubious connections, posited by maverick and daredevil etymologists, are relegated to a separate sentence at the end of certain entries, and this isolation from the bulk of the digested record implies in itself a modicum of skepticism on the part of the compiler (cf. s.v. *drob'*). Only where the conjecture is downright untenable does the author bother to expose it explicitly ("abzulehnen ist": cf. s.v. *drogá*), or to voice his doubt articulately ("weniger überzeugend": s.v. *drévnij;* "unklar": s.v. *dresvá*; "fraglich": s.v. *dristát'*).

(e) The elegant style of allowing the reader to find out for himself about any alternative to the conjecture advocated by the author has already been hinted at on the occasion of an earlier reference to Bender's Lithuanian glossary. Without using any comparably recondite system of encoding, Nielsen, in his Danish dictionary, achieves practically the same effect.

(f) Very full references to earlier writings, with minimal indulgence in acrimonious discussion, are supplied by Wartburg in his *FEW*; also by Hofmann in his revision of Walde's *LEW* — in characteristic and studied contrast to the bibliographically impoverished, but in every other respect deftly tightened presentation of essentially the same facts and issues in Ernout and Meillet's *DÉLL* — with the result that the *LEW* and the *DÉLL* at present constitute a unique pair of mutually complementary etymological treasure troves. The former pours out a more abundant supply of filtered information; the latter affords a higher degree of selectivity and much firmer guidance.

One crucial issue in the organization of an entry is the handling of homonyms (or suspected homonyms, the ever-present alternative being polysemy); the situation is aggravated if the words at issue are also homographs.[10] Some seasoned etymologists, to be on the safe side, operate with a plurality of entries. Thus, C. T. Onions lists six different words *bay* in English, all of them pronounced alike, and distinguishes between them by using numbers: *bay*$_1$ 'bay-tree' (Laurus nobilis) < L. *bāca; bay*$_2$ 'indentation of the sea' < (O) Fr. *baie* beside (O) Sp. *bahía*, cf. Hisp.-L. (Isidore) *baia,* perhaps of Iberian origin; *bay*$_3$ 'opening between columns, etc.; recess' (hence *bay window*) < (O) Fr. *baie*, from *bayer,* earlier *ba-, be-er* 'to gape', Med. L. *batare,* of unknown origin; *bay*$_4$ 'barking of dogs in company,' chiefly (now only) in phrases: *to hold, keep at bay,* older *to turn, bring at a bay,* perhaps from ME *abay* < OFr. (cf. mod. *mettre aux abois*), though there exists an alternative; *bay*$_5$ 'reddish color' < (O) Fr. *bai* < Lat. (Varro) *badiu-s* 'chestnut-colored' (only of horses); *bay*$_6$ 'to bark with a deep voice' < OFr. *abaiier,* It. *(ab)baiare,* from the imitative base **bai-* influenced by *bay*$_4$.

This procession of entries can be reduced from six to five, if one consolidates *bay*$_4$ and *bay*$_6$ rather than being satisfied with the assumption of a secondary contact. The particular sequence in which homonyms are listed can either remain random or be subordinated to chronological (or grammatical) considerations.

The pithy Introduction to the Burrow-Emeneau dictionary (*DED*, pp. xvi-xvii) contains several relevant and very candid paragraphs illustrative of the difficulties this team encountered during the decade or so of their epistolary collaboration. The authors reckon with mergers of words through secondary homophony, as with Telugu *cēru,* and have in such cases resorted to separate listing of the two components (Nos. 1674, 2312). The hazard stems from the existence of putative homophones in Proto-Dravidian, reluctantly allowed because a denial would force analysts to operate with unusual, even improbable connections between two series of meanings for two outwardly similar groups of words, such as 'to be rolled up, coiled, curled; to revolve' vs. 'to shrink, contract, shrivel, grow lean' (even though certain less sophisticated dictionaries, in an effort to amalgamate such conglomerations of words, have gambled on all sorts of *ad hoc* connections). Rival techniques to total merger or strict separation are: the division of heterogeneous entries through punctuation (two short sentences or two short paragraphs rather than a long one); their split into explicitly marked subunits: [a], [b], etc.; and the use of cross-references which "at times mean nothing more than that there are no insuperable phonological objections to connection between the groups, but that the semantic relationship is nothing more than an act of faith." After illustrating their dilemma with such suggestive examples as the 'fish' words vs. the 'flash' words and the 'aerial root' words (as of the banyan) vs. the 'fall, descend' words, the authors pessimistically conclude: "The exact degree of doubt or lack of doubt intended by inclusion, separation, and cross-reference has evaded indication."

Jaberg, in his Introduction (p. xix) to the "propaedeutical dictionary" attached to the *AIS*, also offers, for anyone who aspires to an "einigermaßen befriedigendes Resultat," memorable low-keyed comments, appealing to cultural ("sachlich"), semantic, and areal or geographic considerations and probings. He grants the importance, in such decisions, of the researcher's experience and intuition, and arrives at the following conclusion: "Die Lösung der Aufgabe wird im allgemeinen um so leichter sein, je spezifizierter einerseits der Wortkörper ist und je weniger Bedeutungen ihm anderseits zugeordnet sind. Größere Schwierigkeiten bereiten sehr kurze polysemantische Wörter." In a case of an irreducible margin of doubt, Jaberg, always an advocate of caution, opts for dual listing, with a cross-reference.

The difficulties raised by compounds have already been mentioned in passing. Cumbersome and redundant as the procedure seems at first glance, it may be necessary to include a compound twice, regardless of the chosen perspective. The reader might be disappointed if he does not find Fr. *faux-monnayeur* 'counterfeiter' included under both *faux* and *monnaie* (or, under both *falsus* and *monēta*). But what about affixal derivatives? Unlike many up-to-date standard dictionaries, etymological vocabularies, as a rule, neither "interfile" grammatical morphemes with lexical units, nor display them in a separate alphabetic list — conceivably because there remains a feeling in academic quarters that such information belongs in a treatise on morphology. This deficiency can and, indeed, should be promptly remedied. Meanwhile, one cannot help agreeing with Jaberg (*Index*, p. xix) that derivatives involving a transparent structure and an easily conjecturable meaning (such as diminutives, agentives, and action nouns in Italian) are less worthy of inclusion in a tightly packaged dictionary of word origins than are the items of more intricate architecture.

Similar value judgments apply to interdialectal and intrafamily borrowings. The concept of migratory words is, obviously, very old (what cultured Roman would not have instantly recognized a Hellenism in his own language?) and in isolated cases haunted the imagination of a few seventeenth- and eighteenth-century etymologists (G. Ménage, T. A. Sánchez). From these pioneers the idea, still fairly undeveloped, was inherited by the first generations of comparatists in the past century. Not long after 1900 the full importance of lexical diffusion was recognized, chiefly as a result of the impact of dialect geography; to understand the impetus of the re-orientation it suffices to compare, in regard to a well-chosen slice of material, any edition of Diez's *EWRS* with Meyer-Lübke's *REW*$_1$ (1911-20) and, above all, with his *REW*$_3$ (1930-35). For those scholars who, like W. von Wartburg, dreamed of an etymological dictionary built into a thesaurus (cf. his *FEW*), the opportunities afforded by diffusionist analysis were to be exploited. Other scholars, however, striving toward compactness, saw little wisdom in paying excessive attention to borrowings, except to winnow them out in reconstructions and in the establishment of basic sound correspondences, where they might clutter up operations. Burrow and Emeneau have "tacitly included [a selection of loan-words] in the etymological groups with which they belong" (Introduction to *DED*, p. xvi), but frankly admit that, "to have recorded, and in many instances argued, the borrowing would have swollen the size of the dictionary." This philosophy would apply, *mutatis mutandis*, to the status of Castilianisms in Portuguese and of Lombard words in Tuscan, as seen through the prism of dictionaries of Hispano- and Italo-Romance; but would have no bearing on the labeling of, say, Batavisms and Scandisms in an etymological dictionary of English, an operation which must be carried out without any laxity.

The category of lexical blend or crossing has played an increasingly powerful rôle in etymology. In certain semantic sectors (e.g., kinship terms, numerals, names of parts of the body), on which comparatists have habitually based their claims, such contaminative processes may have been exceptional; in other sectors it is difficult to discover a far-flung family entirely exempt from them. It is possible, though at this juncture unproven, that in certain languages etymologically relevant interferences occur through association with greater frequency than in others; on the other hand, it is demonstrable that, the more thoroughly a field has been plowed under by etymologists, the higher the number of plausible blends. From this situation Meyer-Lübke, sixty years ago, wisely drew the conclusion that, in a typical entry, a special niche should be reserved for blends: He recorded them, especially in the revised edition, after the normal reflexes (cf. Nos. 3779*b*, 3782), before listing any instances of suffix change or back formation or any new derivatives and compounds (3781, 3851), unless, of course, lexical contamination happened to coincide with such derivation and composition (3881). By virtue of this feature of formalization of blends, Meyer-Lübke's dictionary towers over other ventures to which one is tempted to compare it, e.g., Vasmer's *RuEW*.

Once more, at the risk of minor redundancy, the etymologist, to oblige the user of his dictionary, should briefly record contacts, partial blends, and complete mergers of two items under the biographies of both partners, though he will be expected to survey all ramifications of the process on only one occasion.[11]

At the very periphery of even the best-carpentered etymological dictionary one is apt to encounter two unusual categories of entries. The PROVISIONAL entry is one in whose reality (i.e., historical authenticity) even the compiler himself does not believe too firmly. It constitutes a makeshift device for assembling a few pieces of lexical flotsam under one manageable heading, so as to make them eligible for listing in an alphabetic index and to place them, as it were, on tomorrow's etymological agenda. Burrow and Emeneau have included "forms whose phonology is in part at least inexplicable on any basis now known . . . on the chance that they are genetically related and that this can be proved later by intensive study" (*DED*, p. xvi).

An even more controversial class encompasses entries explicitly QUESTIONED or DISCARDED. Thus, Meyer-Lübke, in revising his comparative dictionary (1930-35), altogether eliminated certain bases which had figured in the original edition – a policy which led to gaps in the consecutive numbering of bases.[12] He also added a great many new bases, bearing intercalary numbers (cf. 5808*a*; 6011*a*, 6011*b*, 6011*c*; 6048*a*, 6048*b*; etc.). In a few instances he was willing to list a new base, on the strength of some fellow scholar's advocacy, but in his own comment, appended to the formal listing, he practically revoked the innovation. Thus, he intercalated *plētūra* 'fulness, abundance' out of respect for A. Thomas' plea (No. 6597*a*), but immediately disengaged himself, remarking, apropos OFr. *pleure,* Prov. *pledura*: "Begrifflich nicht verständlich und formell für das Prov[enzalische] . . . bedenklich." Similarly, while yielding to the temptation of introducing, on the advice of some unidentified expert, **panucellus* 'Spinnrocken voll' (No. 6208*b*), he immediately retracted his commitment: "Grödn. [i.e., Central R.-Rom.] *panužel* ist bei der lokalen Beschränkung zweifelhaft."

7

BREADTH

As early as the mid-sixteenth century, one finds etymological dictionaries accompanied by all sorts of prefatory material, supplements, and other features meant to prepare the reader for intelligent consultation of the book or to stimulate his curiosity along parallel lines. Thus, G. Ménage's *Origines* (1650) contains, at the outset, a miniature treatise on historical phonology ("Exemples de la conversion des lettres," pp. i-xxxviii), a practice which is echoed as late (1882) as W. W. Skeat (p. 761); appended to it are not only the expected Additions and Corrections (pp. 665-754), plus a less customary second crop of Additions (pp. 755-845), but also the embryonic form of what would later grow into either an Index Verborum or, under more favorable circumstances, a full-blown *Registerband* containing a two-column list of Latin bases, which takes into account the corpus of the dictionary plus its prefixed phonological sketch and runs to nine (unnumbered) pages, as well as slightly shorter separate alphabetic lists of Italian and Spanish cognates.

Over the years, traditions have developed for optional inclusion of still other features, some of which concern the cataloguer and bibliographer rather than the student of analytical typology.[1] It would be tedious to enumerate and subdivide all the types of lists of abbreviations and bibliographies presently available. Suffice it to state that some formal bibliographies preceding etymological dictionaries (or, less common at present, concluding them) are elaborate to an extreme and represent real treasure troves of clues to technical literatures (Corominas for Spanish, Vasmer for Russian); others are middle-sized and seem to be selective (Meyer for Albanian). In numerous reference works the list of abbreviations and the bibliography have been amalgamated into a single section (by Berneker for Slavic; by Trautmann for Baltic and Slavic; by Jóhannesson for Icelandic). Of structural importance is the unusual procedure, exhibited in a few dictionaries, of lifting all references to technical literature (*Sekundärliteratur*) from the entries (cf. chapter 6) and organizing them as a separate section; e.g., Falk and Torp, rather unconventionally, merged their bibliographic hints with all sorts of stray addenda. A few etymological dictionaries list earlier ventures of this kind (Weekley), sometimes breaking them down according to the languages involved (Nielsen).[2]

One feature that can be crucially important is the preface, provided the author goes beyond doling out bits of trivial "practical advice," recording his debts to fellow scholars who have patiently and scrupulously read his book in manuscript form, or sketching the background of the project. The historian of the discipline — though not necessarily its typologist — will find it singularly rewarding to read the string of prefaces and prefatory notes to consecutive editions of the same standard work — a relatively easy task since the earlier prefaces have frequently been absorbed into later editions (cf. Diez, Skeat, etc.). Thus, the fourth edition (1959-60) of Ernout and Meillet's *DÉLL* contains the authors' separate prefaces to the original edition of 1932, plus the prefatory notes by Ernout, as the surviving partner, to the editions of 1939, 1951, and 1959-60, which all together provide a superb panoramic view of Indo-European and Latin lexicology over a stretch of thirty years.[3] Some prefaces are very substantial; Diez, in launching the *EWRS* (1853), expatiated in his introductory remarks (pp. iii-xxiv) — saturated with innovative ideas — on such matters as phonosymbolism ("Naturausdruck"), folk etymology ("Umdeutung"), doublets ("Scheidewörter" — which he interpreted slightly differently from A. Brachet eight years later), blends, effects of assimilation, dissimilation, and haplology ("Vereinfachung scheinbarer Reduplikation"), etc.; he focused attention on such narrowly circum-scribed but elusive issues as the coinage of postverbal adjectives and nouns; he even broached a few topics which were entirely neglected by his successors (e.g., the characteristic preference granted to *a* in the unstressed opening syllable of a Romance word). While this kind of methodological harvest is a valuable bonus, the use of the preface for the author's settling of accounts with reviewers of an earlier volume, or of the first fascicles of the dictionary is, needless to say, an infelicity, even though the approach was tried by certain celebrities, e.g., by J. Pokorny in the Preface to the Index Volume — prepared by a younger scholar, to boot — of his *IEW*. If the kindling of etymologic polemic by a dictionary is unavoidable, why not reserve a separate pamphlet for it, as did the Batavist J. Franck in his "Streitschrift" *Notgedrungene Beiträge zur Etymologie* (Bonn, 1893), an impassioned rebuttal of Jan te Winkel's earlier acerbic critique of Franck's *EWNT*? Incidentally, Diez had demonstrated — in a separate booklet, of course — how to respond tastefully to such challenges, without resorting to stridency.

As the prototypical example of Ménage has shown, there accrues to the etymologist (or to an associate of his) the special obligation of rescuing from oblivion many lexical items mentioned only incidentally in his dictionary or for some other reason not readily identifiable. Different authors go about this accepted obligation in many ways not easily reconcilable. In the original version (Kristiania, 1903) of their Norwegian-Danish dictionary, Falk and Torp were satisfied with an Old Norse Word Index; but when their book was translated into German as a prerequisite for publication by a Heidelberg firm (1910-11), they agreed to compile a separate Index of German congeners (pp. 1625-1722) – more than twice as long as the original supplement. D. Olivieri's *Dizionario etimologico italiano* (2d ed., 1961) is equipped with an "Indice analitico" (pp. 767-803), which boils down to a list of ca. 2,500 dialect words and numerous foreignisms, principally Gallicisms, for which the author did not deem it appropriate to reserve separate entries on a par with those for standard words; by way of further retrieval of information, Olivieri appends a list of proper names (pp. 804-11) – both toponyms and anthroponyms – that appear briefly in his etymological vignettes.

The "classic" pattern has been to offer a kind of counterview in the Index or *Register,* either prospective or retrospective, to the material displayed in the body of the dictionary. Thus, if the dictionary itself lists ancestral bases as lemmata, the Index will serve as a guide to the respective descendants (or, if these are too numerous to justify complete listing, to an assortment of characteristic descendants); conversely, if the more modern forms constitute the actual entries, the Index will aim at capturing the etyma. Since many prospective dictionaries are programmatically committed to the comparative approach, one would expect to find a richly subdivided Index in a dictionary like Meyer-Lübke's *REW.* Paradoxically, this is not quite the case. The author supplies a single, consolidated list of Romance formations (pp. 815-1153), each localized by an apposite label, followed by separate, distinctly shorter lists of Albanian, Amerindian, Arabic (Hebrew, [Aramaic], Persian), "Asiatic," Basque (and paleo-Iberian), Berber, Germanic, Greek, Celtic (and Ligurian) words, etc., among which he wedges in, in rather absurd fashion, a few columns of proper names (1159-61). In Harry B. Partridge's companion volume to Pokorny's *IEW,* on the other hand, the "classical" pattern – traceable to Bopp's comparative grammar – is beautifully manifest, with the predictable network of major and minor divisions: Indic (Old Indic,

Prakrit, Pali, Neo-Aryan), Iranian (Avestan, Old Persian, Scythian, Sogdian, etc.), and so forth. In retrospective dictionaries which allow for generous mention of cognates, such indexes can be very elaborate. As early as 1891, G. Meyer made a point of assembling, in the "Wortverzeichnis" attached to his Albanian dictionary, separate word lists, not only for the Albanian items which had been obliquely mentioned, but also for Sanskrit, Iranian, Old and Modern Greek, Old Italic, and Romance, with abbreviations of languages by way of tags before individual words where the smallest subdivision was composite ("Slavic," and the like).

On the finer points of inclusion or exclusion, no two authors are likely to coincide completely. Diez, who lived in a time of relative leisure and wrote his $EWRS_1$ (1853) for an élitist, sophisticated readership, was satisfied with a triptych of strictly selective indexes (pp. 748-81: Italian − Spanish/Portuguese − French-Provençal, to the exclusion of [Western] Raeto-Romance and Rumanian). Trying to obviate very time-consuming search, he required his readers to look up Sp. *deslizar* under It. *liscio,* Sp. *desmayar* under It. *smagare,* Sp. *despachar* under It. *pacciare,* Sp. *desmán* under Sp. *ademán,* and Ptg. *enteado* under Sp. *alnado.* Where relationships were simpler, no help was offered; a few minutes of page thumbing was apparently viewed not as an exercise in futility but as a pleasant diversion.

Even before the rise of old-style semasiology, H. Schuchardt's untiring insistence on the semantic or pictorial ingredient of etymological probing honed the sensibility of some lexicographers to varying patterns of meaning. The stage was thus set for the compilation of semantic indexes, a fashion later reinforced through the flowering of dialect geography, which initially throve on onomasiological (or synonymic) maps. Such a key index was somewhat bashfully concealed by Meyer-Lübke under the inconspicuous rubric "Deutsch-Romanisch," which constitutes the sixteenth (and last) division of his Lexical Index. Here the reader learns that, to obtain some initial scraps of information on, say, 'eel,' he should consult the entries *anguīl(l)a, burius, caecus, caput, conger, creare, lamprēda, lancea, pollicāris, wisla.*[4] This is, of course, a miniature exposition of the type of information one finds developed on a grandiose scale in a reference work such as C. D. Buck's *Dictionary of Selected Synonyms in the Principal Indo-European Languages,* conceived as "a contribution to the history of ideas."

The more substantial prefaces − e.g., the one Meillet wrote for the Bloch-Wartburg dictionary − are apt to contain a scattering of methodological nuggets; but it is no longer fashionable to reserve a separate section for a discussion, or bare formulation, of methods, principles, or norms applied in etymological analysis. The situation was different in the past century, when a P. F. Monlau prefixed his "Rudimentos de etimología" to a pioneering genetic dictionary of Spanish, while a W. W. Skeat stated, on two highly concentrated pages (xxi-xxii), his celebrated "Canons for Etymology." A. Nascentes gave a more personal twist to the exposition of such issues by titling the relevant rubric "The Task of the Etymologist" (pp. xiv-xv).

Unlike Ménage — or, in backward Spain of the early nineteenth century, R. Cabrera — the more modern breed of etymologist will balk at including capsulized accounts of historical grammar. Syntax would qualify least of all for consideration. However, certain provinces of morphology — in particular, affixation — can be canvassed as part of the prefatory matter. Amusingly, at least from the angle of the modern observer, Skeat listed the prefixes rather fully (pp. 727-29) in 1882 and examined them in almost lavish detail (pp. 732-36) in his last revision (1909), but devoted just a few paragraphs to the derivational suffixes, alleging their great number to be an obstacle to more adequate treatment.[5] (In a Latin dictionary, the same bias would have been far better justified, inasmuch as most prefixes — *dis-* and *re-* being the major exceptions — also function, independently, as adverbs and/or prepositions, while the suffixes are, as a rule, merely bound forms.) E. Hellqvist's Swedish etymological dictionary included an elaborate prefatory section on "Ordbildning" (pp. i-lxxiii).

An overwrought etymological dictionary may encompass not only historical grammar but also selected elements of language history and glottogeography. To revert to Skeat, that pioneer deemed it necessary to include eight solid pages of "Notes upon the languages cited" (pp. xiii-xx of the 1882 ed.; later revised), almost every note culminating in a reference to "authorities."[6] Today this knowledge is imparted either through textbooks of linguistics or through encyclopedias, which are not allowed to overlap on a major scale with dictionaries; but isolated traces of the older usage subsist — witness the skeletal "Table of Indo-European Languages" in Nielsen's revised Danish dictionary (1969).

There exists a tradition — now obsolescent — for breaking down borrowings according to their numbers, sources, and itineraries, in a balance sheet which may either constitute a separate section or enter into the Preface (or the Introduction, if the book boasts one). Ninety years ago, Skeat, in anticipation of future concern with migratory words, tabulated the vicissitudes of lexical items which English absorbed from other languages, setting down even such complex and often unique routes of diffusion as "French from Latin from Greek from Hebrew from Egyptian," "Portuguese from Ethiopian," "Italian from Malay from Arabic," "French from Italian from Syriac." I find occasional repercussions of this tradition only among the stragglers, e.g., in Nascentes' Portuguese dictionary (pp. xvii-xxxvi), which reflects the tastes of a maverick Brazilian scholar.

If certain optional features of breadth strike one as slightly antiquated — Who today would seriously wish to emulate Skeat's strange predilection, in 1882, for a list of homonyms (pp. 762-71) and one of doublets (pp. 772-74)?[7] — the spirit of modernity has, in turn, left its imprint on the outward configuration of many a newly designed etymological dictionary. If H. Frisk, at the start (1954) of his *GEW*, somewhat awkwardly introduced a provisional preliminary remark and a tentative list of abbreviations (pp. iii-viii), the reason for this extreme degree of caution or even skepticism may very well have been the author's premonition of imposed delays, belated changes of heart, and other events conducive to eventual revision — confusions so clearly manifest in long-drawn-out ventures like Wartburg's almost pathetically overextended *FEW*.

We have so far been concerned, in this chapter, with situations in which certain optional small-scale analyses appear as companion pieces to an elaborately-planned etymological dictionary. One can conceive, however, of radically different structures: an etymological glossary or vocabulary (though seldom a full-blown dictionary) may enter, as a coordinated or subordinated ingredient, into a complexly architectured book. In fact, in an earlier chapter we had occasion to cite, in illustrating just such an arrangement, examples of the etymologically slanted glossaries which used to lend splendor to particularly polished editions of medieval texts (e.g., Menéndez Pidal's *Cid* glossary). Such a hierarchy reappears in other contexts. When K. Duden, in 1893, expanded G. K. Fromman's revision (1877) of F. Bauer's guide to etymology (1859), he produced a book (*Etymologie der neuhochdeutschen Sprache, mit einem ausführlichen etymologischen Wörterverzeichnis*) which is in part a lexically (derivationally and compositionally) tilted historical grammar of German (pp. 3-120) and in part an alphabetically arranged pocket dictionary — a "miniaturized Kluge," as it were. Over against this bipartite scaffolding, with fairly even distribution of talent and space, one discovers all kinds of triptychs, especially with regard to unusual languages, the model being: (a) a small assortment of carefully edited texts, or the chrestomathy ingredient; (followed or preceded by) (b) an outline of historical grammar, which forms the inner core; and (c) a glossary, which may, but need not be, etymological. Such a publication may constitute a reference book or a text, or a free combination of the two genres, any of which will probably bear some such title as *Handbook* ..., or *Manual*....[8] However, there also exist certain recurrent categories of monographs, or loose collections of short papers, in which etymological research – not infrequently dealing with loanwords – is quite likely to be conspicuously represented. Such books are typically recognizable by two alternative patterns of titles: (a) *Armenian Studies,* or, pretentiously Latinized, (b) *Byzantino-Turcica.* True, not all books so titled focus on linguistics, still fewer – within the latter domain – on etymology; some may involve literature, others may cover straight history, or even art history.[9]

The degree of mutual coherence and integration between the component sections of a bi- or tripartite book will, obviously, vary from case to case; pedagogically slanted treatments are bound to exhibit it in higher measure. The Etymological Vocabulary (372-411) which, except for a short "Sachregister" (i.e., Index Rerum, 412-16) concludes the sixth definitive edition (1932) of C. Voretzsch's *Einführung in das Studium der altfranzösischen Sprache* for autodidacts is preceded by (a) a very leisurely word-by-word analysis of the opening laisse of the epic *Pèlerinage de Charlemagne* (5-153); (b) a preliminary digest of the sound correspondences thus far inferred between Latin and Old French (154-94); (c) a linguistic dissection, in ever-quickening tempo, of laisses 2-15 and 50-54 of the same poem (195-268); (d) a cursory systematic survey, in diachronic perspective, of Old French phonology, morphology, and syntax (272-318). These four delicately graded parts and the selective Etymological Glossary, which served as our starting point, clearly form a judiciously integrated whole. The "sampler" of dialectal texts (319-47) and the Bibliographic Supplement (348-71) seem extraneous to the original design.

Generally speaking, the all-important relationship between etymology and historical grammar involves a slightly unstable balance. Volume I (1962-66) of H. Kronasser's *Etymologie der hethitischen Sprache,* for instance, unlike J. Friedrich's counterpart, is not announced as being organized in the form of a dictionary. Of the five fascicles presently available that follow upon the introductory section (devoted, as is customary, to matters of spelling and pronunciation), all seem to be concerned with problems ordinarily dealt with in an elaborate historical grammar. Thus, in §93 the author embarks on his analysis of nominal formations, with a preliminary examination of "radical nouns" (*Wurzelnomina*). A major section (§§94-111) is then devoted to *a*-stems; after certain general remarks and a few comments on their inflection (§94), the author rapidly surveys the primary *a*-stems (§95), so as to reserve the remainder of the section for their suffix-marked counterparts. These are then presented in a no doubt "logical" (presumably alphabetical) sequence, most of them with appropriate subdivisions: the family of *ḫ* suffixes, including *-ḫa-, -ḫša-, -šḫa-* (§96); *-(i)ya (-wiya)* (§97); *-k(k)a-* and *-ane/ika* (§98); *-la-* (§99); *-talla-* and *-tara-* (§§100f.); *-ma-* (§102); *-na-,* with a particularly intricate network of subclasses: *-ana/-anna, -anza(na), -inna,* etc. (§103); *-pa-* (§104); *-šepa- (-nzipa-)* (§105); *-ra-* (§106); *-ša-* (§107); *-ta-* (§108); *-wa-* (§109); *-za-/-nza-* (§110); stems — for the most part of the *a*-class — which sometimes gain, sometimes lose, an *-n-* (§111). The question now arises why this product of filigree work in Hittite philology is passed off as a contribution to etymology rather than to grammar. One reader's impression is, first, that the grammatical pigeonholes established have been filled with lexical illustrations exhaustively rather than selectively as is customary with grammar; and second, that each illustrative example has been filtered with sustained attention to etymological side issues. The result of these two norms is that the entire lexicon of Hittite so far retrieved has been squeezed into the mold of a historical grammar, rather than being presented either alphabetically, i.e., in one routine fashion; or semantically, the most common alternative routine.

8

SCOPE

The most dramatic feature of this parameter (as somewhat arbitrarily defined at the outset) is the oft-observed clash between the demands of pure scholarship and the practical considerations of the publishing business. For the purposes of unadulterated research, the stock of lexical material best qualifying for etymological analysis corresponds to the oldest deposits: pre-Homeric Greek is more valuable than the language of the Attic tragedians, archaic Latin offers the words in more transparent shape than classical Latin (and does not distract the reader's attention through mention of fairly late accretions), Old Spanish is far more relevant to paleo-Romance reconstruction than are Golden Age and modern Spanish. But the exigencies of real life, paradoxically, give greater justification to sponsorship of dictionaries focusing on the later, less pertinent stages of the respective languages. In the massive four-volume dictionary of J. Corominas (*DCE*), medieval Spanish figures prominently on every page, but the entries are all modern Spanish, forcing one to consult one of the appended indexes to ascertain which Old Spanish words alien to the modern lexicon have been smuggled in.[1] The same ailment may befall a historical grammar: What is perhaps most acutely needed is a set of two such grammars, one bridging the gap from Antiquity to the Middle Ages, to the rigorous exclusion of all forms either absent from pre-1400 sources or resistant to any hypothetical projection onto that temporal level. Yet even a scholar as distinguished − in most respects − as the late R. Menéndez Pidal allowed his *Manual de gramática* (though not, of course, his vastly superior *Orígenes*) to be muddied by the gratuitous inclusion of hundreds of postmedieval forms − even where earlier forms should have been close at hand.[2]

At present, it is no longer as certain as it may have been half a century ago that the monumental type of dictionary (a concordance, a thesaurus) is the most suitable context for the formulation and elucidation of etymological issues. (In the data-oriented early twentieth century there was, in some quarters, a feeling − avowed or unacknowledged − that the sheer accumulation of material might lead to a breakthrough in many an impasse.) To be sure, a discreet etymological hint can be an excellent concomitant to a lengthy entry, counterbalancing the massiveness of the record; one associates this prudent policy not only with the *Thesaurus Linguae Latinae* but also with Alcover and Moll's enormously rich Catalan dictionary, as revised by Sanchis Guarner. But Wartburg's idea − conceived around 1920, if not earlier − of merging an exhaustive cross-temporal thesaurus of French literary words plus Gallo-Romance patois formations with a French *etymologicum* seems, in retrospect, to have entailed a considerable overextension of human and archival resources.

The typical etymological dictionary of a modern European tongue just about encompasses the lexicon of the literary language; and, since modern literature – broadly defined – abounds in dialogue (fiction, drama), the colloquial level and even certain lower varieties of the standard language are, as a rule, included. It would be otiose to adduce numerous examples.[3] Even in a culturally advanced territory, such as the European continent and its insular appendages, one encounters pockets where literacy is limited or where another language, or a prestige dialect of the same language, is preferred for the purpose of written communication – a situation in which the etymological dictionary rests preeminently on rural dialectal sources orally tapped. M. L. Wagner's Sardinian dictionary (the *DES*) exemplifies the former situation and the *Glossaire des patois de la Suisse romande* (though etymological only by a stretch of the term) the latter.

There exist a great many examples of unusual or unique delimitations on the scope of an etymological dictionary. Though G. Gröber's "Lateinische Substrate romanischer Wörter" can hardly rank as a dictionary, considering its title and mode of publication (in numerous short installments strung over six annual volumes of a journal), it comes very close to being one,[4] at least a *Supplement-Wörterbuch* of the type made famous by the Provençalists E. Levy and C. Appel in their elaborations on F. Raynouard's pioneering work, except that the distinctive feature of the "Substrate" is the putative character of every single entry. One significant fact, often overlooked, corroborates this interpretation: The "Substrate" were heralded by Gröber's programmatic paper in the opening fascicle of the same short-lived journal: "Sprachquellen und Wortquellen des lateinischen Wörterbuchs" (*ALLG*, I [1884], 35-67), under a title referring explicitly to lexicography. The general climate of the journal, produced by its enterprising, not to say, enthusiastic, editor Eduard Wölfflin, was of course determined by its supporters' intention to lay the foundations for the monumental *Thesaurus Linguae Latinae*. One can embark with equal justification – if less élan – on a dictionary containing no hypothetical bases whatever. This feat could be accomplished, e.g., in Romance, if only words transmitted through learned and semilearned channels were taken into account; the former, by virtue of their sheer transparency, are rather anticlimactic, but the latter, involving all sorts of devious folk etymologies, can be challenging and entertaining, as one gathers at a glance from consultation of H. Rheinfelder's *Kultsprache und Profansprache in den romanischen Ländern* ... (1933) – a classic unsurpassed to this day.

In addition to the supplementary etymological dictionary[5] – exemplified by Caix's (1878) and Thurneysen's elaborations on Diez's *EWRS*, Salvioni's enrichments of Körting's *LRW*, García de Diego's book-length additions to Meyer-Lübke's *REW*, and perhaps "Eduardo de Lisboa" 's malicious pamphlet (1937) inimical to A. Nascentes' Brazilian venture (1933), as well as by Emeneau and Burrow's two-hundred-page Supplement (1968) to their own Dravidian dictionary (1961), plus the forty-page Addenda (1972) to that Supplement – there exist preliminary dictionaries or at least extensive strings of etymological notes conducive to future dictionaries. Examples include J. H. Gallée's *Vorstudien zu einem altniederdeutschen Wörterbuch* (1903) and Th. von Grienberger's *Untersuchungen zur griechischen Wortkunde* (1900), in addition to C. Michaëlis' aforementioned Luso-Hispanic contributions. Restraint or understatement was as characteristic of that period as boisterous flamboyance is of our own.

One important issue is raised by partial dictionaries leaning in the direction of etymologies, i.e., by studies – often conducted on a commendable level of academic excellence and practically never stooping to commercial interests – which examine a slice of the total lexicon, often marshaling the entries in alphabetic order. The size and character of the slice may have been determined by genetic consider-ations; in the overwhelming majority of examples the subject of concern is an assortment of loanwords. The situation is so common-place that there is scarcely any need for copious documentation: For over a century there has been an uninterrupted flow of monographs on such subjects as Germanisms in Lithuanian (K. Alminauskis, 1934); Slavisms, again in Lithuanian (A. Brückner, 1877); Hellenisms in German (F. Dornseiff, 1950); Indo-Aryan words in Dravidian (M. B. Emeneau and T. Burrow, 1962), etc.

Partiality, in a very different sense, is involved if the criterion of discrimination is grammatical rather than ethnoglottic. One of the earliest instances (1873) – after F. Bopp's pioneering efforts – was A. Bezzenberger, *Untersuchungen über die gotischen Adverbien und Partikeln.* K. Brugmann wrote famous monographs of this sort, in the IE perspective, on demonstratives (1904) as well as distributive and collective numerals (1907). J. Endzelin's dissertation (1905), in Russian, investigated Latvian prepositions, etc.

Then again, the fragmentation of the lexicon may be presided over by semantic (or onomasiological) considerations, as when B. Delbrück, as early as 1889, isolated the IE kinship terms for separate consideration, and F. Bechtel, in 1913, launched his ambitious study, *Deutsche Namen einiger Teile des menschlichen Körpers*.

In most of these borderline cases it seems inadvisable to label as a "dictionary" a lexicographic or lexicological monograph bearing on a very idiosyncratic assortment of items. Only where the "strain" under study approaches the variety and diversity of the entire lexicon, through normally proportioned representation of different form classes and semantic (or "real life") domains, does it seem legitimate to classify such a monograph as a special type of dictionary – on condition that the listing of key words be such as one expects to find in a handy reference work. Into this category one could place I. A. Candrea's dictionary of the Latin constituents of the Rumanian lexicon (1907-14, A-P), following upon his Paris dissertation (1902) on the vicissitudes of consonants in Rumanian words of that descent; earlier experiments along the same line are those by A. de Cihac and S. Puşcariu, also, perhaps even with a slight stretch, dictionaries of Arabisms in Hispano-Romance (the best example being the one by W. H. Engelmann and R. Dozy, 1869) and possibly a dictionary of Slavisms in Balkan-Romance.

Finally, there are on record certain marginal varieties of scope. Dictionaries of doublets, which for a while were fashionable in academic quarters and beyond (Brachet, Canello), are etymological by implication if not by definition. Concern with frequency of lexical incidence and curiosity about etymologies are scarcely a good match; nevertheless, abridged etymological dictionaries (Corominas, Nascentes, Uhlenbeck) form some sort of link between these two categories. Humorously styled and erotic dictionaries (*dictionnaires de la langue verte*) seem, at first blush, incompatible, since they cater to entirely different tastes; nevertheless, euphemism and folk-etymological disguise seem to have something in common, and some noted etymologists (A. Scheler, L. Spitzer) have shown strong leanings toward research in *erotica*. Finally, all manner of cant or thieves' argot, which are based on deliberate camouflage, offer challenges to etymological acumen and intuition; it is small wonder that highly competent etymologists, men of unquestionable seriousness, have devoted much time and attention, perhaps even love, to this type of secret language; their roster includes Kluge, Wagner (intermittently), and, above all, the indefatigable Lazare Sainéan. A dictionary of phonosymbolic ("expressive," "iconic") words, inescapably etymological, at least by implication, has at all times been a latent possibility, with which V. García de Diego eventually (1968) decided to busy himself; witness his *Diccionario de voces naturales.*

Distinctly peripheral are dictionaries that are historical, archeological, or geographic, though they often flaunt the word "etymological" in their titles or, at least, discreetly offer incidental bits of etymological information. One example of this comparatively rare category is N. Barsov's medievalistic *Geografičeskij slovar' russkoj zemli,* of very early vintage (1865). Also tangential are the countless onomastic dictionaries, including at least one slanted toward ancient mythology (A. Carnoy, *Dictionnaire étymologique de la mythologie gréco-romaine,* 1937).

One venture very striking when measured by the yardstick of typology is a modern etymological dictionary superimposed on a medieval glossary that was totally unconcerned with word origins. Thus, A. Castro conjoined three Latin-Spanish glossaries — traceable to 1400 or thereabouts — and, in addition to editing them, prepared, in collaboration with J. Corominas and G. Sachs as his silent partners, a composite etymological dictionary (1936), which commands considerable interest, especially if one adds the critical comments by a shrewd if irascible L. Spitzer to the findings of this Madrid team. Conversely, M. Roques published equally valuable Latin-Old French glosses without equipping them with any such etymological apparatus. We have encountered similar instances of expansion of a non-etymological glossary into one adorned with etymological comments in connection with L. Gáldi's (1944) and C. Tagliavini's (1930) editions of older Rumanian vocabularies.

9

PURPOSE AND LEVEL OF TONE

Etymology has sometimes been called the oldest outlet for man's curiosity about language; in any event, its origin precedes by a wide margin the crystallization of historical linguistics as an organized, academically represented discipline; and the existence of a process of associative change often referred to as "folk etymology" is proof that a certain type of etymological interpretation, which manifests itself in the reordering of lexical families or in the assignment of an isolated, "unmotivated" word to a thriving family, can be traced to a milieu of naïve, spontaneous speakers. It is small wonder, under these circumstances, that several other causes in addition to straight scholarship may, at least concomitantly, be served by codification of such knowledge in an etymological dictionary. One major difficulty for the typologist can be described as follows: It seems arbitrary, even hazardous, to draw a razor-sharp line between the serious (objective, truly scientific) and the marginally respectable varieties of etymological research, because useful nuggets of information and even loose threads of felicitous ideas are not infrequently concealed in controversial or downright objectionable (e.g., risqué) books.

The simplest dividing line that one can expect to draw is between (a) deliberately erudite and (b) popular but nevertheless scholarly books. As regards the latter, the seriousness of the enterprise is often implicitly guaranteed by the reputation of the author and the series (or the publishing house). Who, for instance, would question the competence or sincerity of J. Vendryes as the author, in the closing years of his long life (b. 1875), of the *Lexique étymologique de l'irlandais ancien* (A- , M-P; 1959-61)? Certain conclusions can be drawn time and again from the book's title and subtitle. The size of the venture may also yield an indirect clue: massive dictionaries seldom serve as repositories for fantasies or frivolous thoughts. Occasionally the same author (e.g., Wartburg, Corominas) has extracted a shorter and diluted dictionary, cut to fit the needs of lay readers, from a learned one of monumental proportions. Where a dead language is involved, with the possible exception of such widely taught subjects as Greek and Latin, it is practically inconceivable that anything but a serious, professional purpose be intended — though fellow scholars may indeed disagree mildly or even sharply with individual findings, with underlying assumptions, even with the total edifice of the book. Few readers would challenge the intentions of A. J. van Windekens as the author of the *Lexique étymologique des dialectes tokhariens* (1941). One can also wager that, while a Dutch etymological dictionary written in Dutch might conceivably be the work of an amateur or worse (though I am not trying to cast an aspersion on J. Vercouillie's *Beknopt etymologisch woordenboek der nederlandsche taal,* 1890, 1898, 1925), an etymological dictionary of Lithuanian written in German is most unlikely to involve anything but a very technical contribution, such as E. Fraenkel's *Litauisches etymologisches Wörterbuch* (1962-65) is indeed.

It is less easy to reach a clear-cut decision with regard to other categories of etymological dictionaries. L. Sainéan, though not a career academician, applied fully professional standards to the task of ferreting out countless hidden or, at least, not readily accessible slivers of lexical material; he had a flair for etymological connections, an intuitive grasp of plausible sequences of events, and an unusually wide scope of experience, since, for about twenty long years before becoming immersed in problems of French, he had cultivated Rumanian, comparative Romance, and an assortment of Oriental languages. Despite his superb background, commendable accuracy in references and quotations, and exemplary patience, Sainéan, at the moment of decision making, often allowed himself to be swayed by emotional and intellectual whims – through exaggerated allowance for spontaneous creation rather than transmission, for one thing, and through underestimation of the Latin strain of the French vocabulary as against, say, Gaulish, for another.

J. Cejador y Frauca's etymological writings deserve to be placed one notch below those of Sainéan. A tireless reader of recondite books – many of them unavailable outside Madrid – he amassed enormous collections of lexical *fiches,* but his determination to achieve completeness of information was not matched by his meticulosity on the more tedious levels of research, such as the faithful copying of the passages quoted or the exact identification of the *loci.* In addition to these shortcomings, Cejador entertained very bizarre ideas about the background of Spanish, constantly aggrandizing the rôle played by Ibero-Basque and belittling the part of the Graeco-Latin heritage. Despite this combination of flaws and manifestations of haste and prejudice, on Cejador's part, the prime sources he tapped are so copious and, more often than not, so unusual as to justify cautious consultation of his writings, including the posthumous *Vocabulario medieval castellano* (which marks the nadir of elementary tidiness), but to the virtual exclusion of his explicative efforts.

Outside the domain of those objectionable dictionaries which were, at least, sincerely meant to serve the advancement of knowledge, one must place certain lexicographic ventures, a few of them with built-in etymological sections, which cater to enlightened diversion. The problem of the relation of pure cognition to witty and ingenious entertainment is an intricate one and far transcends the province of linguistics, but since bizarre word histories and humorous, especially piquant, ambiguities are presumably the two bridges which link the world of language to the world of laughter, etymological guides to the language of the underworld and to *erotica* (for the sake of both the omnipresent *double entendre* and of lexical items banished from the standard dictionaries due to considerations of decorum or prudery) do exist and must sometimes be taken into account for serious purposes.

10

CONCLUSION

The typological analysis here presented lends itself to several uses. One might construct from it a system of coding that would describe very briefly but without omitting any significant feature the design, level, prime purpose, etc., of any etymological dictionary. Taken in this narrowly utilitarian sense, the typology could compete with – or, rather, supplement – a catalogue, bibliography, chain of abstracts, or similar reference tool, representing the far more analytical approach because it would expose and highlight many concealed features, which an experienced linguist rather than a professional librarian can best detect.

One is free to imagine more exciting uses. If hundreds of etymological dictionaries have been compiled in the past, there is no reason to doubt (unless one altogether despairs of the future of historical linguistics) that an even higher number of such books are yet to appear. The author of any such future venture certainly has a right, perhaps even an obligation, to canvass his options. Of course, etymologists have, traditionally, used to good advantage writings – including those of dictionary format – by their predecessors, whether in the same subfield or in adjoining subfields. Gamillscheg, in the Preface to the *EWFS,* professed his admiration for the Germanist Kluge, but he is unlikely to have spurned the opportunity to consult as well the books by his immediate forerunners Brachet, Clédat, Scheler, Littré, and the Darmesteter-Hatzfeld-Thomas team. However, the author of a Norwegian dictionary will seldom find the leisure to open a

Sanskrit or a Persian dictionary, unless he is at work on some exotic word — and, if he does, he will focus his attention on the "message" (i.e., the particular etymological verdict) rather than on the structure of the book, still less on the implications of that structure. A typological survey allows, indeed invites, a newly initiated etymologist to assess his best chances of bold strategy before the plunge into a quicksand of tiny facts and petty commitments. This potential didactic (or, as Karl Jaberg might have said, propaedeutic) value of the typological approach seems to me more worthy of esteem than the strictly pragmatic dividends it pays, or at least is capable of paying.

One envisages a still higher level of stimulus, beyond immediate application. While dictionaries, in the context of our culture, rank — perhaps excusably — as an uninspiring, even pedestrian category of book, and while, possibly as a result of that reputation, highly imaginative etymologists (Hugo Schuchardt, for one) have consistently shrunk from any temptation to compile such an inventory of genetic solutions and impasses, all linguists constantly use such books, and many very fine scholars (a Diez at the dawn, a Meillet in the past, a Frisk in our own days) have made a point of composing one. Through such dictionaries, ideas and data are funneled into the brain chambers of even those scholars who themselves refuse to write tedious reference works and prefer instead to experiment freely with and through less restricted genres of investigation: monographs, articles, notes, essays, and searching book reviews. Etymological dictionaries, in other words, indirectly nourish some of the most imaginative varieties of linguistic research, and since a typological survey borders on a partial critique of an entire genre, several essential or casual observations here made could be interpreted as being relevant to etymology as a whole — in particular, to the active acquisition, rather than mere codification, of etymological knowledge.

The system of parameters, or dimensions, here chosen — in imitation of earlier analyses bearing on historical grammars or on dictionaries of any kind — represents nothing complete, definitive, or exclusive. It marks an attempt to subsume the largest possible number of stray organizational remarks under the smallest possible number of general considerations, the ideal, probably unattainable in practice, being to avoid redundancy as consistently as possible. Nevertheless, the presentation here set forth is unlikely to be free from overlaps: certain comments have been repeated, not necessarily through inadvertence (though I have striven, in such instances, to vary at least the illustrations).

A matter entirely different from repetition (whether through a lapse or on purpose) is the interlocking – or, to use a different metaphor – the affinity of certain dimensions. Thus, the choice of a "prospective" array for a dictionary, as here defined – i.e., the decision to make the dictionary start either from a putative or from a philologically accessible parent language – carries with it significant implications that transcend the temporal perspective. One expects from a dictionary of this type a certain plateau of tone and from its author a certain professionalism which one would, to be sure, also welcome in a book and in a scholar offering a "retrospective" counterview, but which, under a new set of conditions, might no longer appear nearly-obligatory. By the same token, features of "breadth" and of "scope" may closely coincide and even condition each other.

Typological critique, implicit in a survey, must not aspire to supplanting other types of assessment. While we have not completely eliminated value judgments relating to workmanship, we have introduced them only parenthetically – in a few contexts perhaps for the sake of amenity, subordinating them to other criteria of relevance. Thus, it is highly pertinent that Meyer-Lübke devised a sophisticated pattern for the structure of an entry in a comparative etymological dictionary; the facts that he did not consistently live up to his own ideal, or that the data he garnered show glaring lacunae, or that the bibliographic and typographic filtering of the information conveyed was not carried out with the expected punctilio, are not crucially important in the perspective of typology, though they may substantially detract from the value of his book when it is judged from other angles. The assessment of an author's actual performance must remain the preserve – and the privilege – of the individual book review, on whose territory typology must not trespass. Again, the prerogatives of the history of a discipline must be carefully safeguarded, since typology is neither synchronic nor diachronic, but panchronic – or, if you prefer, achronic. For this very reason, it is not inconceivable that some dictionary entirely antiquated in every other respect may capture the attention of the typologist through some long-overlooked original feature of structure; or that the value of a modern book condemned in general by critics may be partially redeemed if an ingredient of its organization can be shown to deserve adoption. Thus, if a scale of values emerges at all in typological analysis, it may be radically at variance with the yardsticks used in better-known traditions of measurement.

It goes without saying that no quick combination of, say, features *x, y,* and *z* picked as particularly desirable from a typological survey such as ours guarantees per se the successful manufacturing of any "synthetic" etymological dictionary. Certain elements of taste, perspective, experience, knack for styling and verbalization, even typographic refinement must in most instances be added before a masterpiece comes into existence. Very seldom has such a dictionary been fathered by any young, or even young middle-aged, person – a circumstance which gives pause, because linguistics in general surely has had no lack of precocious geniuses, if not downright child prodigies. But an etymological dictionary constitutes, essentially, a venture in diachronic research and is, as such, more closely akin to experiments in history than in mathematics. Now, the attainment of the highest plateau of achievement in historiography coincides, as a rule, with advanced maturity rather than with youth, conceivably in contrast to the breakthroughs accomplished in mathematical sciences. Moreover, any dictionary – even one slanted in the direction of word origins – remains, for better or worse, a reference work and presupposes, on the part of its compiler, a certain dosage of patience and dispassionateness in covering, here and there, unexciting patches of territory. Finally, an etymologist, to sound convincing, must have accumulated and absorbed a respectable knowledge of countless nonlinguistic facts, a time-consuming investment of energy. The reader notices at once, even from short hints, Ernout's superb command of Roman literature, Mitzka's firm grasp of German *Kulturgeschichte,* and similar manifestations of multifaceted expertise. All these imponderable ingredients, which lend a diversity of pleasant flavors to the best specimens of etymological lexicography, militate against the adoption of any "crash" program in the engineering of etymological dictionaries.

On balance, then, typology is at its most helpful and least obnoxious in isolating transferable elements of organization and execution, i.e., those which lend themselves to abstract formulation and to enlightening discussion out of their immediate context. These universals in the strategy and tactics of the codification of etymological inquiry, must, at every juncture, be balanced against features of uniqueness – equally arresting, yet, as a rule, far more elusive.

NOTES

CHAPTER 1

1. The major earlier studies include the articles "A Tentative Typology of Etymological Studies," *IJAL*, XXIII (1957), 1-17; "Distinctive Features in Lexicography: A Typological Approach to Dictionaries Exemplified with Spanish," *RPh*, XII (1958-59), 366-99, and XIII (1959-60), 111-55; and "A Tentative Typology of Romance Historical Grammars," *Lingua*, IX (1960), 321-416; to these may be added, as a germane exploration, the lecture "Distinctive Traits of Romance Linguistics" (1959), which was eventually absorbed into the miscellany *Language in Culture and Society,* ed. D. Hymes (New York, etc., 1964), pp. 671-86, and figures, furthermore, in *Readings in Romance Linguistics,* ed. James M. Anderson and Jo Ann Creore (The Hague–Paris, 1972), pp. 13-38. A drastically reduced version of the second item appeared under the title "A Typological Classification of Dictionaries on the Basis of Distinctive Features," *IJAL*, XXXVIII:2 (1962), Part IV (*Problems in Lexicography*), ed. F. W. Householder and S. Saporta, pp. 3-24; there exists a second ed. (1967), slightly revised, of the *Problems.* Some of these papers, brought up to date, figure in two collections of my articles: *Essays on Linguistic Themes* (Oxford, 1968) and *Linguistica generale – Filologia romanza – Etimologia* (Firenze, 1970). For a list of critical reactions to all these experimental studies see *AEM*, VI (1969 [-71]), 609-39.

2. This type of research fascinated the late Berkeley Sinologist Peter A. Boodberg. One finds echoes of that curiosity in a highly original Master's thesis he directed: William G. Boltz, *Archaic Chinese Initial Consonant Cluster* *BS (1969). Here, in slightly condensed form, is the opening paragraph of Boltz's Conclusion (p. 80 of typescript): "We have adduced basically two kinds of data: individual characters, including their phonological and graphic structures; and bisyllabic expressions, some of which are atomic binoms, while others are pleonastic compounds composed of two free words. On the basis of a semantic common denominator, we have postulated a relationship

between all the individual data, monosyllables and bisyllables alike, in the form of a word family, or logoplast with a phonological shape."

CHAPTER 2

1. Compilations of this type were sometimes referred to as "comparative philological dictionaries"; cf. the title of Matías Calandrelli's monumental project, of which only a torso survived (1880-83). While the handling of the etymological facet may appear almost disreputable to moderns, it generated at the time a good deal of enthusiasm, speculation, and discussion. Cf. A. Navarro Viola's pamphlet, available at the British Museum: *Juicio crítico del Diccionario filológico comparado de la lengua castellana* (1884) — fundamentally, a comparative assessment of Barcia's and Calandrelli's pretentious dictionaries.

2. As I have attempted to show in a lengthy review of the first two fascicles of the *Thesaurus* (see *Lang.*, XLVII [1971], 465-87), this book seems to move in the direction of a string of monographs, in which case the title is a misnomer. Even so, the author's total *œuvre* — ever since his memorable contribution to the Jud Testimonial (1943) — comes close to representing a (chaotically organized) dictionary of substratal bases.

CHAPTER 4

1. Between L. Diefenbach and S. Feist one can place, along the chronological axis, G. H. Balg's *Comparative Glossary of the Gothic Language,* which also commands a certain local interest as a specimen of early Americana (1887-89). As an (undistinguished) example of early Rossica one may cite N. Gorjaev's *Sravnitel'no-ètimologičeskij slovar'* ... (1896) and a supplement to it emblazoning the same key words in its title (1901). Still different in its controlled use of comparatism is W. Prellwitz's *Etymologisches Wörterbuch der griechischen Sprache, mit besonderer Berücksichtigung des Neuhochdeutschen* (1892, 1905); preference is overtly given to the readers' native tongue. As regards comparative grammars, the norm is exemplified with C. Bartholomae's "Kurzgefasste vergleichende Grammatik," which enters as a prime constituent into his *Handbuch der altiranischen Dialekte* (1883), and, long before, by the *Vergleichende Grammatik* ... (1833-42; 2d ed., 1857-61; 3d ed., 1868-71) from the pen of Franz Bopp — who, incidentally, also expanded his modest *Glossarium Sanscritum* (1830; 2d ed., 1847) into a distinctly more ambitious *Glossarium comparativum linguae Sanscriticae* (1867). The most judicious label for a comparatively tilted grammar of a single language that has come to my attention appears on the title page of the second, thoroughly recast version (1965) of M. Mayrhofer's *Sanskrit Grammatik mit*

vergleichenden Erörterungen; the original edition (1953) lacked the elaboration. A less carefully circumscribed title was chosen by E. H. Sturtevant for his *Comparative Grammar of the Hittite Language* (1933; 2d ed., revised by E. Adelaide Hahn, 1951).

CHAPTER 5

1. In close proximity to the standard etymological dictionary are various marginal types of lexicological (or broadly linguistic) monographs characterized by patterns of titles suggestive and often informative as to the sources tapped and the ground covered, but inexplicit as to the chosen approach: *Origines Europaeae* (L. Diefenbach), *Germania Romana* (T. Frings) and, in inverse distribution, *Romania Germanica* (E. Gamillscheg); also, *Byzantino-Turcica* (G. Moravcsik), etc.

Another group of investigations aims at all sorts of auxiliary, ancillary, tentative, provisional, preliminary collections of lexico-etymological data or else offers, by way of companion volume, a list of suggested corrections and additions in reference to a major book — occasionally one by the same author, as with G. Alessio, 1962 (the latter category, strictly speaking, constitutes the extreme case of an overextended book review). Cf., on the one hand, N. Barsov's *Materjaly dlja slovarja* ... (1865) and C. Bartholomae's *Zum altiranischen Wörterbuch: Nacharbeiten und Vorarbeiten* (1906) and, on the other, R. Thurneysen's *Keltoromanisches; die keltischen Etymologien im "EWRS" von F. Diez* (1884).

Certain authors, through the use of "glossary" or "index" rather than "dictionary," announce the modesty of their aim, which may be to provide an etymologically annotated short or partial word list. Cf. G. I. Ascoli's *Glossarium palaeohibernicum* ("ordinato etimologicamente e con intenti comparativi") and, in the United States, H. H. Bender's *Lithuanian Etymological Index* (1921). A certain selectivity and freedom from constraint is further implied by such a hazily circumscribed title as A. Ernout's *Aspects du vocabulaire latin.*

A residue of titles are, of course, so loosely worded as to leave a wide scope for the inclusion of miscellaneous literary, folkloristic, linguistic, and straight historical inquiries; here the name of the series or the sponsoring institution, in addition to the author's own reputation, may provide a much-needed clarification. Examples in point are J. Endzelin's *Slavjano-baltijskije ètjudy* (1911), E. Lidén's *Armenische Studien,* G. Meyer's *Albanesische* and *neugriechische Studien* (1883-96, 1894-95), H. Petersson's *Baltisches und Slavisches* (1916) — bizarrely echoing J. J. Mikkola's monograph (1903) published under the very same title — beside the Swedish scholar's *Arische und armenische Studien* (1920).

In general, titles in this domain are not entirely reliable guides. Thus, G. Devoto's *Avviamento all'etimologia italiana* happens to be a "fancy" title for a medium-sized dictionary (as a factual subtitle helpfully makes clear), while G. Curtius' *Grundzüge der griechischen Etymologie,* long-authoritative (especially after its revision by E. Windisch), embodies a venture not at all lexicographically arranged.

CHAPTER 6

1. It suffices to contrast Hofmann's self-contained entry *ankôn* 'elbow' with Frisk's far more comprehensive counterpart *ank-:* The Swedish scholar neatly distinguishes between combinations with the -*l*-, the -*n*-, the -*r*-, the -*s*-, and the -*tro*- suffixes, then sets off two adverbs and refers to a dubious (i.e., philologically spurious) trace of an additional elaboration through the -*ā*- suffix.

2. Let me quote a few characteristic passages from the Introduction: "Repräsentativ sind in unserem Falle die Stichwörter, wenn sie die zahlreichen auf den Karten verzeichneten lautlichen Gestaltungen desselben Etymons unter einer einfachen und leicht lesbaren Etikette zusammenzufassen. Dieser Forderung ist leicht zu genügen, wenn ein übergeordnetes schriftsprachliches Wort zur Verfügung steht. . . . Wenn ein solches fehlt, . . . haben wir eine Kopfform gewählt, die dem supponierten Etymon möglichst nahe steht, möglichst weit verbreitet ist" (p. xviii).

The two following pages contain comments on issues raised by homonymy and by affixal derivation and candidly allow for ceaseless conflicts between scientific rigor and practical concerns.

Jaberg's worries about standardization ("Typisierung") have not been sufficiently appreciated by the critics of the *Index* and by later workers; for one isolated attempt at elaboration see my paper "Etymology and General Linguistics", *Word,* XVIII (1962), 198-219, at 217f.; included in *Essays on Linguistic Themes* (Oxford, 1968), pp. 175-98.

3. The last point is noteworthy, because the most recent currents of linguistics and of literary criticism seem to converge in the rôle of the reader or listener (interlocutor) as that of the co-conditioner of the performance of the writer or speaker, both of them eager for some response if not necessarily for uncritical acceptance.

4. I can cite, at random, from the revised 2d ed. (1950), such instances as *combinaison* (s.v. *combiner*), established in 1680, but tried out, as it were, by Oresme in the fourteenth century; *comice,* borrowed by the fourteenth-century translator, Bersuire, with the sense of 'place of Roman assembly'; used after 1694, in the plural, for the assemblies themselves; and truly naturalized ca. 1760 when the term came to designate certain agricultural reunions in Anjou; etc. The revisers of

Dauzat's dictionary pour in such information in even stronger dosages; thus, one learns that *image*, in the eleventh century, was used for 'statue,' in the twelfth for 'portrait,' and in the mid-sixteenth for 'symbol,' while *imagination* at first suggested 'hallucination,' later 'vision,' and only with Montaigne (ca. 1580) acquired its present meaning. In each instance, microscopic inquiry (which, even where it is available, can hardly be epitomized in a compact dictionary) may alone show whether three separate borrowings from Cl. *imāgō* and Late L. *imāginātiō* are involved or whether internal semantic growth within French is at issue (the two processes may also have interlocked). In any event, Dubois and Mitterand were wise to alter the original title of the Dauzat dictionary, calling it instead "étymologique et historique."

The problems raised by a straight historical dictionary invite a separate discussion, which cannot be provided here. Cf. Ashok R. Kelkar, "The Scope of a Historical Dictionary," in: *Studies in Historical Sanskrit Lexicography* (Poona: Deccan College, 1973), pp. 57-69, with a schematic "Anatomy of a Historical Dictionary Entry" appended to the discussion (p. 68); and such general treatises as L. Zgusta, *Manual of Lexicography* (Praha, 1971), pp. 200-202.

5. Thus, by combing just eight pages of his Sanskrit dictionary (II, 152-59), one discovers the following spirited reactions: "nicht sicher geklärt," "also wohl," "freilich müβte . . ., doch kann . . .," "wohl nicht zufällig ähnlich," "weiteres ist unklar," "etwa . . . was natürlich unsicher bleibt," "ohne gesicherte Deutung," "wünschenswert wäre," "wäre also immerhin vorstellbar," "kann aber nicht recht überzeugen," "sehr unglaubhaft," "es liegt also der Verdacht nahe," "doch kann die Möglichkeit nicht geleugnet werden," "jedenfalls nicht so glatt," "wenig glaubhaft," "nicht über jeden Zweifel erhaben," "sehr konstruiert," "nicht vorzuziehen," "ist trotz B. . . . kaum ererbt," "der Ursprung ist nicht sicher bestimmt," "möglicher Zusammenhang," "völlig abwegig," "etymologisch (ganz) unklar," "fälschlich deduziert," "nicht ganz sicher," "vielleicht (trotz gewissen lautlichen Schwierig-keiten)," "mit erwägenswerten Gründen," "besteht schwerlich ein Zusammenhang," "Anschlüsse ungesichert," "nicht überzeugend," "sicher verfehlt."

A few readers may, of course, disapprove of such lavish and subjectively-colored verbal orchestration and would have preferred a leaner and more abstract (numerical?) system of rating the plausibility of each proposal.

6. I regret to report an almost anachronistic perpetuation, in the United States, of the pointless habit of supplying etymologies in glossaries to textual editions and to chrestomathies, despite C. Carroll Marden's and H. Keniston's praiseworthy efforts to the contrary; the latest example that has come to my attention is the revised second

edition (1973) of the *Anthology of Provençal Troubadours* by R. T. Hill and T. G. Bergin. Only in the case of texts very unusual on the lexical side, such as the medieval veterinary treatise *El libro de los caballos*, ed. Georg Sachs (Madrid, 1936), or the Aljamiado Koran translation (ed. Consuelo López-Morillas; California at Berkeley dissertation, 1974), is this policy defensible.

7. The full list can be excerpted from the bibliography ushering in the posthumous testimonial volume (*Homenagem* . . ., 1930). The main thrust of her attack stretches from the "Studien zur romanischen Wortschöpfung" prepared for the *Miscellanea Caix-Canello,* pp. 113-60, to the two splendid "Contribuïções para o futuro dicionário etimológico . . ." (*RL*) of the years 1908 and 1910.

8. The tradition which required that the glossary to a medieval text, to achieve high-quality ranking, include a restatement of old etymologies and, if at all possible, the discovery of new ones reached its zenith in R. Menéndez Pidal's monumental *Cid* edition (1908-11); interestingly, the author left only the glossary, of all sections, unrevised in 1944-46. Significantly, C. Carroll Marden included etymological identifications in his — all told, superficial — glossary to the *Poema de Fernán González* (1904), but omitted them from the splendid vocabulary that accompanied his sophisticated edition of the *Libro de Apolonio* a decade or so later. On the front of Old French studies, the policy adopted by L. Foulet in his masterly companion volumes (1927, 1955) to J. Bédier's *Roland* edition and to W. Roach's edition of *The Continuations of the Old French "Perceval"* . . . marks a retreat from idle etymologizing. A workable compromise was chosen by M. Rodrigues Lapa in the glossary bound — despite separate pagination — with his edition of Old Galician-Portuguese *Cantigas d'escarnho e de mal dizer:* No etyma are supplied, but certain words — though not all that could have qualified — are discreetly identified as borrowings from Old French or Old Provençal; cf. such entries as *alhor, avol, barnage,* . . . (Why not *ardido* as well?)

9. It is hardly necessary to emphasize the fact that some influential, oft-quoted etymological dictionaries have been mere appendages to critical editions of texts, i.e., strictly constituents of the exegetic apparatus, on a par with footnotes, etc. This restriction holds for É. Ernault's *Dictionnaire étymologique du breton moyen,* attached to the compiler's edition and translation (1885-87) of the Breton tragic play *Le mystère de Sainte Barbe* (1557).

10. This particular issue ties in with the broader question of the treatment of homonyms, partial homonyms, and homographs in lexicography. Relatively few authors of modern bilingual dictionaries have made a policy of amalgamating all such "look-alikes"; one case in point is Holt's bidirectional *Spanish and English Dictionary,* compiled

by Edwin B. Williams. There exists a whole body of literature on the theoretical foundation of this broader issue, divorced from etymology. For a competent and up-to-date digest turn to L. Zgusta, *Manual of Lexicography* (Praha, 1971), pp. 74-89; a more personal approach, in conjunction with polysemy, prevails in Josette Rey-Debove's *Étude linguistique et sémiotique des dictionnaires français contemporains* (The Hague – Paris, 1971), pp. 129, 163f., 168; cf. my review in *Language Sciences,* No. 37 (October 1975), pp. 29-33.

11. On this facet of his policy I find even Meyer-Lübke – despite his generally high level of formality – rather inconsistent. Thus, under *lōtium* 'urine,' he posits a blend with *lutum* 'dirt' to justify Campid. *luttsu* 'urine' (the Sardinian word perpetuates the medial consonant cluster of the former base and the stressed vowel of the latter); but under *lutum* one looks in vain for any hint or cross-reference. Thus, while Meyer-Lübke devised an excellent scheme for his entries, he did not, as a practitioner, adhere too faithfully to his own blueprint.

12. It might some day be rewarding to inquire into the rationale behind such belated omissions. Under the letters N, O, and P – selected at random for inspection – one finds several such lacunae: 5812, 5815, 5830, 5839, 5907, 5918, 5922, 5932, 5933, 5958, 6019, 6049, 6063, 6085, 6089, 6120, etc.

CHAPTER 7

1. Such details as the inclusion of Errata, not infrequently paired off with Addenda (as in the 1882 ed. of Skeat, pp. 775-99), are of scant interest; so are last-minute additions, which F. Holthausen, in his Old English dictionary, distinguished from the bulk of the Supplement ("Nachlese" vs. "Nachträge"); biographical memoirs of the author – written by his successor or, in the case of Ernest Weekley (1865-1954), by his son, on the occasion of the 1967 reprint of the 1921 dictionary; explanations of the typographic symbols adopted (Holthausen, in his aforementioned book, reserved five pages for this sole purpose), and the like.

2. In otherwise routine reprints of earlier editions, money-wise publishers have sometimes made an exception for the formal Bibliography, allowing some younger workers to bring it up to date after the death of the original author. This is what H. Ch. Matthes and his student assistant W. Kühlwein have accomplished, at the request of the C. Winter firm, when the latter reissued in 1963 Holthausen's Old English dictionary (orig. date: 1934).

3. Revisers, understandably, often mention typical additions they have made to the earlier text, and W. Mitzka's remarks in his Prefaces to the seventeenth (1957) and eighteenth (1959) editions of Kluge's *EWDS* are no exceptions from this rule. But in 1957 Mitzka

also reported — a unique admission — that he had made certain cuts, omitting three categories of words: (a) exotic foreignisms that had failed to strike root in German (*Feluke, Pilaw, Samun*); (b) exceedingly narrow regionalisms, such as *Sente;* (c) dialectally tinged zoonyms and phytonyms (e.g., *Kalitte*), since the alternative to deletion in the last class would have been acceptance of other such items by the hundreds.

4. Incidentally, it was G. Körting — an otherwise disreputable etymologist — who used the device of a semantic index (1891, 1901, 1907) long before Meyer-Lübke (1920).

5. Even stranger, from today's vantage point, is Skeat's "List of [461] Aryan Roots" (pp. 729-46), followed by a brief Index, at least in the original edition (p. 747). Of course, whole treatises of historical grammar were sometimes prefixed to dictionaries in the nineteenth century (one immediately recalls A. Darmesteter's book-length presentation of French in the *Dictionnaire général* or F. A. Coelho's treatment of Portuguese in Volume I of Vieira's *Grande Dicionário* . . .). But the two dictionaries just mentioned were not primarily etymological.

6. This procedure led, unavoidably, to a certain overlap with the formal Bibliography, greatly expanded in the revised edition (pp. xxx-xli).

7. This particular bit of evidence might be added to the dossier I drew up in an editorial comment: "One Short-Lived Genre of Glottohistorical Research" (*RPh,* XXVI [1972-73], 749-51), and in a brief note (to appear in a forthcoming Testimonial Volume): "The Analysis of Lexical Doublets; the Romanists' Earliest Contribution to General Linguistics." See also "Conflicting Prosodic Inferences from Ascoli's and Darmesteter's Laws," *RPh,* XXVIII (1974-75), 483-520.

8. Typical tripartite books of the kind here referred to are: J. Endzelin, *Lettisches Lesebuch: Grammatische und metrische Vorbemerkungen, Texte und Glossar* (1922), and J. Franck, *Mittelniederländische Grammatik mit Lesestücken und Glossar* (1883, 1910). Conceivably the earliest example is F. Justi, *Handbuch der Zendsprache. Altbactrisches Wörterbuch, Grammatik, Chrestomathie* (1864). Grammar (or phonology) and etymology are, of course, more closely enmeshed with each other than either is with an anthology or a chrestomathy, with the result that a bipartite structure has also come into existence, exemplified, on the one hand, by H. Hübschmann, *Etymologie und Lautlehre der ossetischen Sprache* (1887), and, on the other, by N. Jokl, *Studien zur albanesischen Etymologie und Wortbildung* (1911), according to whether the scholar in charge has placed heavier emphasis on phonology or on morphology. Jokl's range of interests corresponds to that brilliantly exhibited by the Romanist A. Thomas.

9. The Swedish scholar E. Lidén (who used German as his

92

favorite medium) showed a strong predilection for the *Studien* . . . type of miscellany, advancing from his *Studien zur altindischen und vergleichenden Sprachgeschichte* (1897) via *Armenische Studien* (1906) to *Studien zur tocharischen Sprachgeschichte* (1916), though he did not spurn the alternative of such a bifocal title as *Vermischtes zur Wortkunde und Grammatik* (1891-94), from which D. J. Georgacas has not deviated much in preparing his "Grammatische und etymologische Miszellen zum Spät- und Neugriechischen" (1951). Note also H. Pedersen's *Études lituaniennes* (1933). By omitting *Studien,* or *Beiträge,* or *Vermischtes* one arrives at such a label as *Zur slavischen und vergleichenden Wortschöpfung,* by H. Peterssen (1915). Fairly close to the latter is Max Niedermann's *Essais d'étymologie et de critique verbale latines* (1918), though Niedermann was posthumously honored by a collection of his shorter papers (1956) bracketed under the title *Balto-Slavica,* as against Herbert Petersson's earlier (1916, 1918) *Baltisches und Slavisches* and *Baltische und slavische Wortstudien.*

On account of their haziness such key words in the titles as *Grundriß* or *Grundzüge* were fashionable for a while – but are no longer favored. P. Horn's *Grundriß der neupersischen Etymologie* (1893) was sufficiently close to the dictionary category to justify its inclusion in C. Winter's prestigious series "Sammlung indogermanischer Wörterbücher"; and it was sufficiently weighty to induce a scholar of H. Hübschmann's caliber to write a series of *Beiträge,* which enter, together with the younger worker's *Neupersische Lautlehre,* into a separate volume, *Persische Studien* (1895). On his own, Hübschmann launched a series *Armenische Studien,* the opening fascicle (1883) of which was, not unexpectedly, *Grundzüge der armenischen Etymologie.* It will be remembered that S. Feist, as a beginner (1888), struck out with a *Grundriß der gotischen Etymologie* (1888), which only later was metamorphosed into a corresponding *Etymologisches Wörterbuch* . . . (1909, 1920-23) and, eventually, into a *Vergleichendes Wörterbuch.* . . .

CHAPTER 8

1. Even this operation is far from easy, since one is forced to look up the item under scrutiny, in Volume IV (1957), under the general rubric of "Grupos léxicos," under "[Unusual] Arabisms" (pp. 1100c-1a); Mozarabisms (pp. 1104b-5a); passages of medieval texts commented upon in a lexicological key (pp. 1106c-7c); words culled from certain standard reference works, e.g., historical grammars, comparative etymological dictionaries (including the *FEW* and the *REW*), and linguistic atlases (pp. 1107c-15a); and then to continue the search under the separate rubric of "Índices de palabras," again under "Mozarabic" (pp. 1115a-9c), "Portuguese and Old Galician-

Portuguese" (pp. 1119c-35b), "Catalan" (pp. 1135b-54a), "Provençal = Lengua de Oc" (pp. 1154a-59), "Latin and Primitive (= Common) Romance" (pp. 1175c-93b), etc. Amid all these intricacies and tokens of sophistication, Corominas has apparently forgotten to compile the one list that might have been truly functional: the index of obsolete Spanish formations which were only obliquely examined. Of course, the exceptional reader who is really eager to ascertain the author's verdicts on select Old Spanish etymologies now has access to J. Corominas' heavily annotated edition (1967) of the *Libro de buen amor* (ca. 1330) by Juan Ruiz — a book equipped with an elaborate analytical index (pp. 637-67), which provides helpful clues to philologically tinted lexical notes.

2. Thus, in §5 bis — where, after the introductory statements, the formal historical analysis picks up momentum — Menéndez Pidal cites *quince* 'fifteen' and *árbol* 'tree,' instead of *quinze* and *árvol*. In §6 he brings in *tinieblas* 'darkness' and *hijuelo* 'young child,' also *beodo* 'drunk,' *buítre* 'vulture,' *desahúcia (desáucia)* 'gives up hope,' *decía* '(s) he said,' etc., even though the truly helpful links between the parent language and contemporary Spanish would unquestionably have been *te-* or *ti-niebras, fijuelo, bebdo, bueytre, desafúzia,* and *dezía*. In this respect a book otherwise distinctly inferior to Menéndez Pidal's *Manual,* namely A. Zauner's *Altspanisches Elementarbuch* (1908, 1921), by virtue of a stricter programmatic confinement to Old Spanish, is a shade more reliable. Attempts to bridge the gap between older and more modern Spanish have, incidentally, been discouragingly few; A. Alonso's *De la pronunciación medieval a la moderna en español* and H. Keniston's *Syntax of Castilian Prose* come to mind — both of which were doomed to remain mere torsos.

3. Abundant documentation from *belles-lettres* is, understandably, most characteristic not of straight etymological dictionaries, but of mixed, multipurpose ventures, such as Littré's and Darmesteter-Hatzfeld's for French and the Royal Academy's and Cuervo's for Spanish. The standard etymological dictionary is chiefly concerned with *Erstbelege* and, increasingly, with the far more elusive *Letztbelege;* literary sources are also tapped (e.g., in the *FEW*) as evidence of semantic or stylistic shifts.

4. Note the unusual meaning of "substratum." There also exist a few older dictionaries dealing with residues of archaic languages and thus coming distinctly closer to our present concept of "substratum." One example is the "Lexicon der von den Alten aufbewahrten Sprachreste der Kelten und ihrer Nachbarn," included in Lorenz Diefenbach's *"Origines Europaeae." Die alten Völker Europas mit ihren Sippen und Nachbarn* (1861).

5. On the Germanic side one notes C. B. van Haeringen's

250-page *Supplement* (1936) to Johannes Franck's *Etymologisch woordenboek der nederlandsche taal* (1892), as revised by N. van Wijk (1912-29) — a cycle of activities which was closed with the compilation of a third edition (1949) of the Franck dictionary, this time revised by van Wijk and van Haeringen.

ABBREVIATIONS AND SYMBOLS

I. STANDARD REFERENCE WORKS

AFW   *Altfranzösisches Wörterbuch,* by A. Tobler and E. Lommatzsch

AIS   *Sprach- und Sachatlas Italiens und der Südschweiz,* by K. Jaberg, J. Jud, et al.

DCE   *Diccionario crítico etimológico de la lengua castellana,* by J. Corominas

DED   *Dravidian Etymological Dictionary,* by T. Burrow and M. B. Emeneau

DEEH   *Diccionario etimológico español e hispánico,* by V. García de Diego

DEI   *Dizionario etimologico italiano,* by C. Battisti and G. Alessio

DÉLF   *Dictionnaire étymologique de la langue française,* either by A. Dauzat or by O. Bloch and W. von Wartburg

DÉLL   *Dictionnaire étymologique de la langue latine,* by A. Meillet and A. Ernout

DES   *Dizionario etimologico sardo,* by M. L. Wagner

EWDS   *Etymologisches Wörterbuch der deutschen Sprache,* by F. Kluge

EWFS   *Etymologisches Wörterbuch der französischen Sprache,* by E. Gamillscheg

EWNT   *Etymologisch woordenboek der nederlandsche taal,* by J. Franck

EWRS   *Etymologisches Wörterbuch der romanischen Sprachen,* by F. Diez

FEW   *Französisches etymologisches Wörterbuch,* by W. von Wartburg

GEW   *Griechisches etymologisches Wörterbuch,* by H. Frisk

IEW   *Indogermanisches etymologisches Wörterbuch,* by J. Pokorny [and H. B. Partridge]

Abbreviations and Symbols

LEW	*Lateinisches etymologisches Wörterbuch,* by A. Walde and J. B. Hofmann
LRW	*Lateinisch-romanisches Wörterbuch,* by G. Körting
NDÉH	*Nouveau dictionnaire étymologique et historique,* by J. Dubois and H. Mitterand
REW	*Romanisches etymologisches Wörterbuch,* by W. Meyer-Lübke
RuEW	*Russiches etymologisches Wörterbuch,* by M.Vasmer
ThLL	*Thesaurus Linguae Latinae,* orig. sponsored by five German Academies; ed. J. B. Hofmann
VWIS	*Vergleichendes Wörterbuch der indogermanischen Sprachen,* by A. Walde and J. Pokorny

II. Periodicals and Monograph Series

AEM	*Anuario de Estudios Medievales*
AGI	*Archivio Glottologico Italiano*
ALLG	*Archiv für lateinische Lexikographie und Grammatik*
BCSFLSic	*Biblioteca del Centro di studi filologici e linguistici siciliani*
BÉHÉ	*Bibliothèque de l'École des Hautes Études*
BSLP	*Bulletin de la Société de Linguistique de Paris*
GHÅ	*Göteborgs Högskolas Årsskrift*
IF	*Indogermanische Forschungen*
IJAL	*International Journal of American Linguistics*
JSFO	*Journal de la Société Finno-Ougrienne*
Lang.	*Language*
LUÅ	*Lunds Universitets Årsskrift*
RFE	*Revista de filología española*
RL	*Revista Lusitana*
RPh	*Romance Philology*
SGEH	Sammlung germanischer Elementar- und Handbücher
ZfPh	*Zeitschrift für Phonetik und allgemeine Sprachwissenschaft* (later: ... *Phonetik, Sprachwissenschaft und Kommunikationsforschung*)
ZFSL	*Zeitschrift für französische Sprache und Literatur*

III. Languages and Dialects

Anglo-L.	Anglo-Latin, i.e., medieval Latin as used in England
Campid.	Campidanese (southern Sardinian)
Celt.	Celtic
Ch. L.	Church Latin
Cl.	Classical (Latin)

Corn.	Cornish
Cymr.	Cymric
E.	English
Fr.	French
Friul.	Friulano or Friulian (= Eastern Raeto-Romance)
Frk.	Frankish
G.	German
Gmc.	Germanic
Goth.	Gothic
Gr.	Classical Greek
Gr.-L.	Graeco-Latin
Hisp.-L.	Hispano-Latin
IE	Indo-European
It.	Italian
L.	Latin
Late L.	The Latin of declining Antiquity and transition to Middle Ages
MBr.	Middle Breton
MDu.	Middle Dutch
ME	Middle English
Med. L.	Medieval Latin
MHG	Middle High German
MLG	Middle Low German
OFr.	Old French
OHG	Old High German
OSp.	Old Spanish
pre-IE	preceding any stage of Indo-European
proto-IE	representing the primitive stage of Indo-European
Prov.	(Old) Provençal, the medieval literary language of southern France
Ptg.	Portuguese
R.-Rom.	R(h)aeto-Romance
Russ.	Russian
Sanskr.	Sanskrit
Sp.	Spanish

IV. BIBLIOGRAPHIC AND SCHOLARLY TERMS: ENGLISH

comp.	compiled, compiler
dir.	directed by
Diss.	dissertation
ed.	edited by, editor
fasc.	fascicle
fig.	figuratively
lit.	literally

mod.	modern
MS	manuscript
orig.	original(ly)
OT	Old Testament
pl.	plural
pseud.	pseudonym
repr.	reprinted
rev.	revised
SE	Southeast
Ser.	Series
sg.	singular
Suppl.	Supplement
s. v(v).	sub verbo (verbis), see under the word(s)
Univ.	University
unpubl.	unpublished

V. BIBLIOGRAPHIC AND SCHOLARLY TERMS: FOREIGN

Abh.	Abhandlung(en)
Akad. der Wiss. (van Wet., etc.)	Akademie der Wissenschaften
archéol.	archéologique
Bibl.	Bibliothek (Bibliothèque, etc.)
Fac.	Faculté (Fakultät, etc.)
Germ.	germanisch
hist.	historique
Hist.-Philos. Kl.	Historisch-philosophische Klasse
Sitz.-ber.	Sitzungsberichte
Soc. de Ling.	Société de Linguistique (de Paris)
Succ.	Successore (etc.)

VI. SYMBOLS

$\sqrt{}$	root [obsolete symbol]
X	lexical blend, crossing, contamination
*	hypothetical form
[*]	form which should have been marked as hypothetical
>	conducive to, yielding [a more recent form]
<	extracted from, cast off by [an older form]
→	transmitted into (from one language to another)

Subscript numerals either distinguish homonyms and, especially, homographs or mark editions of certain reference works, e.g., REW_3 = revised third edition of W. Meyer-Lübke's *Romanisches etymologisches Wörterbuch*.

BIBLIOGRAPHY

This Bibliography serves a dual purpose: the obligatory one of acting as a frame of reference for the monograph (text and notes) to which it is appended; and the optional one of providing clues to other etymological dictionaries so far neither touched upon nor even mentioned in passing. This complex function explains why, in addition to authentic etymological dictionaries, representatives of some other genres of tangential relevance to the typologic survey have been included. Space limitations and considerations of balance must justify (or, at least, excuse) the omission of numerous titles which, unquestionably, would have deserved inclusion in any straight bibliography.

It has seemed to me worthwhile to record, wherever pertinent, several consecutive editions of certain successful works, especially where not just new printings but attempts at genuine revision were involved. This kind of information is far from otiose; it allows one to draw inferences as to the fluctuating taste of the reading public; to measure the reception of a particular book and of a style of research – even a type of curiosity; to follow the intellectual development, even the avatars, of an individual author; and, most important from the angle of typology, to recognize at a glance the possible characteristic varieties of etymological dictionaries, vocabularies, and glossaries. Changes in the titles of certain books may also act as eye-openers.

Cross-references have been provided on a minimal scale, particularly in cases where a later work was explicitly planned as an elaboration on, or a refutation of, an earlier venture; and references to significant appraisals are furnished only under exceptional circumstances.

In compiling the Bibliography I have tapped – in a less than truly methodic fashion – diverse sources: catalogues of research libraries, book-review sections of learned journals, bibliographies – not infrequently generous ones – ushering in some of the best among the available dictionaries.

My own familiarity with the sources cited varies greatly. Several dictionaries have accompanied me over a period of thirty to forty years; I have even personally known the authors of quite a few (Gamillscheg and Vasmer happened to be my teachers in Berlin throughout the mid-thirties). In other instances I made an effort to familiarize myself with books little known to me until then from personal experience. Under unfavorable circumstances, I have, not without hesitation, included in the list certain items which I had never actually consulted and thus observed "in action" or through testing. In domains far removed from my own specialty, I have occasionally relied on the verdicts of authoritative fellow scholars.

Alcover, Antoni M., & Francesch de B. Moll. *Diccionari català-valencià-balear; inventari lexical y etimològich de la llengua que parlen Catalunya espanyola....* 10 vols. Palma de Mallorca, 1930-62. 2d ed., Vols. I-II, 1964-68.

Alessio, Giovanni. *L'elemento greco nella toponomastica della Sicilia.* 2 vols. Biblioteca del Centro di studi filologici e linguistici siciliani, V, XIII. Firenze: Sansoni, 1954-56.

––––––. "Nuove postille al *Dizionario Etimologico Italiano.*" *BCSFLSic,* VI (1962), 59-110.

––––––. *Saggio di toponomastica calabrese.* Biblioteca dell' "Archivum Romanicum," II: 25. Firenze: L. S. Olschki, 1939. See also under Battisti, Carlo.

Alminauskis, Kazimieras. *Die Germanismen des Litauischen.* I: *Die deutschen Lehnwörter im Litauischen.* Diss. Leipzig, 1934-35.

Alonso, Amado (†1952). *De la pronunciación medieval a la moderna en español,* ed. Rafael Lapesa. Biblioteca Románica Hispánica, I:5. 2 vols. Madrid: Gredos, 1955-69. Rev. ed. of Vol. I, 1967.

Andriotes, N[ikolaos] P. Ἐτυμολογικὸ λεξικὸ τῆς κοινῆς νεοελληνικῆς. 2d ed., Thessalonike: Institut d'Études Néohelléniques, 1967.

Appel, Carl. See under Levy, Emil.

Arendt, Carl. See under Bopp, Franz.

Ascoli, Graziadio Isaia, ed. "Glossarium palaeohibernicum." *AGI,* VI (1879), pp. xvii-cccviii [Supplement dated 1888].

Baldinger, Kurt, et al. *Dictionnaire étymologique de l'ancien français.* Québec: Les Presses de L'Université Laval, 1971-.

Balg, G. H. *A Comparative Glossary of the Gothic Language....* Maryville, Wis., and New York: B. Westermann & Co., 1887-89.

Barcia, Roque. *Primer diccionario general etimológico de la lengua española.* 5 vols. Barcelona: Seix, 1880-83. Repr., Buenos Aires, 1945. Cf. under Navarro Viola, A.

Barsov, Nikolaj. *Materjaly dlja istoriko-geografičeskogo slovarja Rossii.* I: *Geografičeskij slovar' russkoj zemli (IX–XIV st.)* (Wilna: Syrkin, 1865).

Bartholomae, Christian. *Altiranisches Wörterbuch.* Straβburg: K. J. Trübner, 1904. Repr., Berlin: W. de Gruyter, 1961.

––––––. *Handbuch der altiranischen Dialekte. Kurzgefaβte vergleichende Grammatik, Lesestücke und Glossar.* Leipzig: Breitkopf & Hartel, 1883.

––––––. *Zum altiranischen Wörterbuch. Nacharbeiten und Vorarbeiten.* Beiheft zu *IF,* XIX (ed. K. Brugmann & W. Streitberg). Straβburg: K. J. Trübner, 1906.

––––––. *Zur Etymologie und Wortbildung der indogermanischen Sprachen.* Sitz.-ber. Heidelberg, X:10. Heidelberg: C. Winter, 1919.

Battisti, Carlo, & Giovanni Alessio. *Dizionario Etimologico Italiano.* 5 vols. Firenze: G. Barbèra, 1950-57.

Bauer, Walter. *Griechisch-deutsches Wörterbuch zu den Schriften des Neuen Testaments und der übrigen urchristlichen Literatur.* 3d ed. ("völlig neu bearbeitet"). Berlin: A. Töpelmann, 1937 [originally, in 1925, a rev. of E. Preuschen's older dictionary]. 4th ed., 1952. 5th ed., 1958. Tr. by W. F. Arndt & F. W. Gingrich: *A Greek-English Lexicon of the New Testament....* Chicago: University of Chicago Press, 1957. (New ed. in press.)

BIBLIOGRAPHY

Beauquier, Charles. *Vocabulaire étymologique des provincialismes usités dans le Département de Doubs.* Besançon, 1881.

Bechtel, Friedrich. *Deutsche Namen einiger Teile des menschlichen Körpers.* Halle: Waisenhaus, 1913.

──── *Die historischen Personennamen des Griechischen bis zur Kaiserzeit.* Halle: M. Niemeyer, 1917.

──── *Lexilogus zu Homer. Etymologie und Stammbildung homerischer Wörter.* Halle: M. Niemeyer, 1914.

Bender, Harold H. *A Lithuanian Etymological Index.* . . . Princeton University Press, 1921.

Benveniste, Émile. *Le vocabulaire des institutions indo-européennes,* ed. Jean Lallot. 2 vols. Paris: Éditions de Minuit, 1969. Tr. by Elizabeth Palmer: *Indo-European Language and Society.* Miami Linguistics Series, XII. Coral Gables: University of Miami Press, 1973.

Bergin, Thomas Goddard, & Raymond Thompson Hill, comps. *Anthology of the Provençal Troubadours.* 2 vols. 2d ed. ("revised and enlarged with the collaboration of S. Olson, W. D. Paden, Jr., and N. Smith"). Yale Romanic Studies, II:23, New Haven & London: Yale University Press, 1973. Glossary: II, 104-245. (Original ed.: Yale Romanic Studies, XVII, 1941.)

Berneker, Erich. *Die preußische Sprache; Texte, Grammatik, etymologisches Wörterbuch.* Straßburg: K. J. Trübner, 1896. (Part of the item appeared in 1895 as a Leipzig dissertation.)

──── *Slawische Chrestomathie mit Glossaren.* Straßburg: K. J. Trübner, 1902.

──── *Slawisches etymologisches Wörterbuch.* 2 vols. A – Mor- (incomplete). Sammlung slavischer Lehr- und Handbücher, dirs. A. Leskien & E. Berneker, II:1-2. Heidelberg: C. Winter, 1908-13. Repr. 1924.

Bertoldi, Vittorio. *Un ribelle nel regno de' fiori; i nomi romanzi del "Colchicum autumnale L." attraverso il tempo e lo spazio.* Bibl. dell' "Archivum Romanicum", II: 4. Genève: L. S. Olschki, 1923.

Betz, Werner. See under Paul, Hermann.

Bezzenberger, A. *Untersuchungen über die gotischen Adverbien und Partikeln.* Halle: Waisenhaus, 1873 (diss. Göttingen).

Bloch, Jules. *La formation de la langue marathe. BÉHÉ,* CCXV. Paris: H. Champion, 1915.

Bloch, Oscar. *Lexique français-patois des Vosges méridionales.* Paris: H. Champion, 1915 [i.e., 1917]. Supplements the author's *Atlas linguistique des Vosges méridionales* (1917) and includes a chapter on "Noms de lieux" (pp. 145-54).

──── In collaboration with W. von Wartburg. *Dictionnaire étymologique de la langue française.* Preface by A. Meillet. 2 vols. Paris: Les Presses Universitaires de France, 1932. Rev. 2d ed. (in 1 vol.), 1950. Rev. 3d ed., 1960. Rev. 4th ed., 1964. Rev. 5th ed., 1968.

Böhtlingk, Otto, & Rudolf Roth. *[Petersburger] Sanskrit-wörterbuch.* 7 vols. St. Petersburg: Kaiserliche Akademie der Wissenschaften, 1855-75. (The dictionary also exists in a shorter version, 1879-89, reissued in 1923-25, and accompanied by *Nachträge,* ed. R. Schmidt, Leipzig: O. Harrassowitz, 1928.)

Boisacq, Émile. *Dictionnaire étymologique de la langue grecque, étudiée dans ses rapports avec les autres langues indo-européennes.* Heidelberg: C. Winter,

1916. 2d ed., Heidelberg: C. Winter, and Paris: C. Klincksieck, 1923. 3d ed., 1938. 4th ed. ("augmentée d'un index par Helmut Rix"), 1950.

Boltz, William G. "Archaic Chinese Initial Consonant Cluster *BS–." Master's thesis, Oriental Languages, University of California, Berkeley, 1969. Typescript, 87 pp.

Bolza, G. B. *Vocabolario genetico-etimologico della lingua italiana.* Vienna: Stamperia di Corte e di Stato, 1852.

Bopp, Franz. *Glossarium Sanscritum.* Berlin: F. Dümmler, 1830. Rev. 2d ed.: *Glossarium Sanscritum in quo omnes radices et vocabula usatissima explicantur et cum vocabulis Graecis, Latinis, . . . comparantur,* 1847. Rev. 3d ed.: *Glossarium comparativum linguae Sanscriticae, in quo vocabula Sanscrita accentu notata sunt Latinisque litteris transcripta; adiecti sunt indices,* 1867.

———. *Vergleichende Grammatik des Sanskrit, Zend, ...* 4 vols. Berlin: F. Dümmler, 1833-42. 2d ed. ("gänzlich umgearbeitet"), in 3 vols., 1857-61. Rev. 3d ed., 1868-71. There exist translations: by M. Bréal into French (based on the 2d German ed.), and by E. B. Eastwick into English (3d ed., 1862). Index vol.: Carl Arendt, *Ausführliches Sach- und Wortregister zur 2. Auflage.* Berlin: F. Dümmler, 1863.

Bouda, Karl. *Baskisch-kaukasische Etymologien.* Bibl. der allgemeinen Sprachwissenschaft, Series III. Heidelberg: C. Winter, 1949.

———. "Baskisch und Kaukasisch." *ZfPh,* II (1948), 182-202, 336-52.

———. *Die Beziehungen des Sumerischen zum Baskischen, Westkaukasischen und Tibetischen.* Mitteilungen der altorientalischen Gesellschaft, XII:3. Leipzig: O. Harrassowitz, 1938.

———. *Der Dual des Obugrischen, mit einem Exkurs über die Suffixlockerheit.* Diss. Berlin, 1933. Extracted from the *JSFU,* XLVII (1934).

———. *Lakkische Studien.* Heidelberg: C. Winter, 1949.

———. *Neue baskisch-kaukasische Etymologien.* Acta Salmanticensia: Filosofía y Letras, V:4 (1952).

———. *Nombres vascos de las plantas,* tr. Luis Michelena. Ibid., VII:3 (1955).

———. *Die Verwandtschaftsverhältnisse der tschuktschischen Sprachgruppe: Tschuktschisch, Korjakisch, Kamtschadalisch.* Ibid., V:6 (1952).

Brachet, Auguste. *Dictionnaire des doublets, ou doubles formes de la langue française.* Paris: A. Franck, 1868. Supplément, 1871.

———. *Dictionnaire étymologique de la langue française.* Preface by E. Egger. 9th ed., Paris: J. Hetzel [187-]; 15th ed., 1880. Tr. into English by G. W. Kitchin. 3d ed., Oxford: Clarendon Press, 1882.

Brückner, Alexander (Aleksander). *Die slawischen Fremdwörter im Litauischen.* Litauisch-Slawische Studien, I. Weimar: W. Böhlau, 1877.

———. *Słownik etymologiczny języka polskiego.* Kraków: Nakładi i Własność Krakowskiej Spółki Wydawniczej, 1926-27. 2d ed., with a Preface by Zenon Klemensiewicz, Warszawa: Wiedza Powszechna, 1957.

Brugmann, K. *Die Demonstrativa der indogermanischen Sprachen.* Abh. der Sächsischen Akademie, XXII:6. Leipzig, 1904.

———. *Die distributiven und die kollektiven Numeralia der indogermanischen Sprachen.* Ibid., XXV:5 (1907).

Buck, Carl Darling. *A Dictionary of Selected Synonyms in the Principal*

Indo-European Languages; a Contribution to the History of Ideas. Chicago: University of Chicago Press, 1949.

Burrow, T[homas], & M[urray] B. Emeneau. *A Dravidian Etymological Dictionary.* Oxford: Clarendon Press, 1961.

———. *Supplement.* Oxford: Clarendon Press, 1968. "Dravidian Etymological Notes, Parts I-II." *Journal of the American Oriental Society,* XCII (1972), 397-418, 475-91.

Cabrera, Ramón (†1833). *Diccionario de etimologías de la lengua castellana,* ed. J. P. Ayegui. 2 vols. Madrid, 1837.

Cahen, Maurice. *Études sur le vocabulaire religieux du vieux-scandinave: la libation.* Collection linguistique, IX. Paris: É. Champion, 1921.

Caix, Napoleone. *Studi di etimologia italiana e romanza; osservazioni ed aggiunte al "Vocabolario etimologico delle lingue romanze" di F. Diez.* Firenze: G. C. Sansoni, 1878.

Calandrelli, M. *Diccionario filológico comparado de la lengua castellana.* Preface by V. F. López. 5 vols. (A–Co). Buenos Aires: "Obras clásicas," 1880-82 ['83].

Candrea (-Hecht), (J.) A. *Les éléments latins de la langue roumaine; le consonantisme.* Thèse, Université de Paris. Paris: E. Bouillon, 1902.

———. *Dicţionarul limbii române din trecut şi de astăzi* (incorporated into the *Dicţionarul enciclopedic ilustrat "Cartea românească,"* by A. C. and Gh. Adamescu, Bucureşti [1931]).

———, & O. Densusianu. *Dicţionar etimologic al limbii române; elementele latine (A-Pu).* Bucureşti: 1907-14.

Canello, U. A. "Gli allòtropi italiani." *AGI,* III (1878), 285-419.

Carnoy, Albert. *Dictionnaire étymologique de la mythologie gréco-romaine.* Louvain: Universitas, 1957.

Castro, Américo. *Glosarios latino-españoles de la Edad Media.* Suppl. XXII to *RFE.* Madrid, 1936. Cf. under Spitzer, Leo.

Cejador y Frauca, Julio (†1927). *El lenguaje; sus transformaciones, su estructura, su unidad, su origen, su razón de ser; estudios por medio de la comparación de las lenguas.* 12 vols. Madrid, 1902-14.

———. *Vocabulario medieval castellano.* Madrid: Hernando, 1929.

Chambers, William (†1883; publisher?). *Chambers's Etymological Dictionary of the English Language; a New and Thoroughly Revised Edition,* ed. A. Findlater. London & Edinburgh: W. & R. Chambers, 1900. New ed., 1963. (An edition credited to James Donald is traceable to 1872).

Chang Hsüan. *The Etymologies of Three Thousand Chinese Characters in Common Usage.* Hong Kong University Press, 1968. Cf. review by Paul L.-M. Serruys, *Journal of Chinese Linguistics,* I:3 (1973), 479-92.

Chantraine, Pierre. *Dictionnaire étymologique de la langue grecque: Histoire des mots.* Paris: Klincksieck, 1968-.

Cihac, A. de. *Dictionnaire d'étymologie daco-romane,* I: *Éléments latins comparés avec les autres langues romanes;* II: *Éléments slaves, magyars, turcs, grecs-moderne et albanais.* 2 vols. Francfort s.M.: L. St. Goar, 1870-79.

Cioranescu, Alexandre. *Diccionario etimológico rumano.* 2 vols. Biblioteca Filológica. La Laguna: Universidad, 1958-66.

Clédat, Léon. *Dictionnaire étymologique de la langue française.* 14th ed. Paris: Hachette, 1917.

Coelho, Francisco Adolfo. *Dicionário manual etimológico da língua portuguesa, contendo a significação e prosódia.* Lisboa: P. Plantier, ca. 1890.

———. *A língua portuguesa: fonologia, etimologia, morfologia e sintaxe.* Coimbra: Imprensa da Universidade, 1868.

Corblet, Jules. *Glossaire étymologique et comparatif du patois picard.* Paris, 1851.

Corominas, Joan (Juan). *Breve diccionario etimológico de la lengua castellana.* Biblioteca románica hispánica, V:2. Madrid: Gredos, 1961. Rev. 2d ed., 1967. 3d ed., 1974.

———. *Diccionario crítico etimológico de la lengua castellana.* 4 vols. Biblioteca románica hispánica, V. Madrid: Gredos, and Bern: A. Francke, [1954-57]. Repr. ca. 1970. Cf. under Gillet, Joseph H., and Spitzer, Leo.

———. Ed. Juan Ruiz, *Libro de buen amor.* Biblioteca Románica Hispánica, IV: Textos. Madrid: Gredos, 1967.

Covarrubias (H)orozco, Sebastián de. *Tesoro de la lengua castellana o española.* Madrid: L. Sánchez, 1611. 2d ed., by M. Sánchez, in 2 vols., 1673-74, with addenda by P^e Benito Remigio Noydens. Crit. ed. by M. de Riquer, Barcelona: Horta, 1943.

Cuervo, Rufino José. *Diccionario de construcción y régimen de la lengua castellana.* 2 vols. (A–D). Paris: A. Roger & F. Chernoviz, 1886-93. Repr., Bogotá: Instituto Caro y Cuervo, 1953-54. (Parts of the material pertaining to the letter E-, arranged in fascicles, have appeared in Bogotá, sometimes also as articles in the journal *Thesaurus;* fasc. 5, corresponding to pp. 340-400, is dated 1974.)

Curtius, Georg. *Grundzüge der griechischen Etymologie,* I. Leipzig: B. G. Teubner, 1858. 5th ed., rev. in collaboration with Ernst Windisch, 1879.

Darmesteter, Arsène, coauthor with A. Hatzfeld and A. Thomas. *Dictionnaire général de la langue française, du commencement du XVIIe siècle jusqu'à nos jours.* 2 vols. Paris: C. Delagrave, 1890-1900. 6th ed., 1920.

Dauzat, Albert. *Dictionnaire étymologique de la langue française.* Paris: Larousse, 1938. 7th ed., 1947. 10th ed., "avec un supplément lexicologique et un supplément chronologique," 1949, 1954.

———. *Dictionnaire étymologique des noms de famille et prénoms de France.* Paris: Larousse, 1951. 3d ed., rev. by Marie-Thérèse Morlet, 1960.

———. *Les noms de famille de France; traité d'anthroponymie française.* Paris: Payot, 1945.

———. *Les noms de lieux, origine et évolution; villes et villages – pays – cours d'eau – montagnes – lieux-dits.* Paris: Delagrave, 1926. 2d ed., 1928.

———. *La toponymie française.* Bibliothèque scientifique. Paris: Payot, 1939. Rev. ed., 1960.

———, Jean Dubois, & Henri Mitterand. *Nouveau dictionnaire étymologique et historique.* Paris: Larousse, 1964. (Revision of *DÉLF,* above.)

———, & Charles Rostaing. *Dictionnaire étymologique des noms de lieux en France.* Paris: Larousse [1963].

Delbrück, Berthold. *Die indogermanischen Verwandtschaftsnamen.* Sächs. Akad. der Wiss., Sitz.-ber. XI:5. Leipzig, 1889.

Densusianu. Ovid. See under Candrea-Hecht.

BIBLIOGRAPHY

Devic, L. Marcel. *Dictionnaire étymologique des mots français d'origine orientale (arabe, persan, turc, hébreu, malais).* Paris: 1876. Repr. Amsterdam: Oriental Press, 1965. Also published as part of Émile Littré's dictionary.

Devoto, Giacomo. *Avviamento alla etimologia italiana. Dizionario etimologico.* Firenze: F. Le Monnier, 1966. 2d printing, 1967.

Diefenbach, Lorenz. "Lexicon der von den Alten aufbewahrten Sprachreste der Kelten und ihrer Nachbarn." In *Origines Europaeae: Die alten Völker Europas mit ihren Sippen und Nachbarn.* Frankfurt, 1861.

———. *Vergleichendes Wörterbuch der gotischen Sprache.* 2 vols. Frankfurt, 1851.

Diez, Friedrich (†1876). *Etymologisches Wörterbuch der romanischen Sprachen.* Bonn: A. Marcus, 1853. 2d ed., 1861. Rev. 3d ed., 2 vols., 1869-70. 4th ed., with a Supplement by A. Scheler 1878. 5th ed., with a revised Supplement by A. Scheler, 1887. Cf. Jan Urban Jarník, *Index zu Diez' "EWRS"* [4th ed.], Heilbronn: Henninger 1878. Id., *Neuer vollständiger Index zu . . .* [5th ed.], 1889. See also under Caix, Napoleone, and Thurneysen, Rudolf.

Dornseiff, Franz. *Der deutsche Wortschatz nach Sachgruppen.* Berlin & Leipzig: W. de Gruyter, 1934. 5th ed., Berlin, 1959.

———. *Die griechischen Wörter im Deutschen.* Berlin: W. de Gruyter, 1950.

———. *Rückläufiges Wörterbuch der deutschen Eigennamen.* Berlin: Akademie-Verlag, 1957.

Dozy, R[einhart]. *Dictionnaire détaillé des noms des vêtements chez les Arabes.* Amsterdam: J. Müller, 1845.

———. *Oosterlingen. Verklarende lijst der Nederlandsche woorden, die uit het Arabisch, Hebreeuwsch, Chaldeewsch, Perzisch en Turkisch afkomstig zijn.* 's-Gravenhage: M. Nijhoff, 1867.

———. *Supplément aux dictionnaires arabes.* 2 vols. Leyde: E. J. Brill, 1881. 2d printing, 1927. 3d printing, 1967. Cf. under Engelmann, W. H.

Du Cange, Charles Du Fresne, Sieur. *Glossarium ad scriptores mediae et infimae graecitatis.* Lyon: Anissonios, J. Posuel, & C. Rigaud, 1688. Repr. Vratislaviae, 1891; Paris: Collège de France, 1943; Graz, 1958.

Duden, Konrad. *Etymologie der neuhochdeutschen Sprache, mit einem ausführlichen etymologischen Wörterverzeichnis* [pp. 121-72], "zugleich 3. Aufl. von Bauer-Frommanns *Etymologie.*" Münster, 1893. (Friedrich Bauer's original edition: 1859; G. K. Frommann's revision: 1877.) Cf. under Grebe, Paul.

Echegaray, Eduardo de. *Diccionario general etimológico de la lengua española.* 5 vols. Madrid: J. M. Faquineli, 1887-89.

"Eduardo de Lisboa" [pseud.]. *O Dicionário do Sr. Nascentes e o "REW"; Rectificações.* Rio de Janeiro: Pimenta de Mello, 1937.

Eguílaz y Yanguas, Leopoldo. *Glosario etimológico de las palabras españolas (castellanas, catalanas, gallegas, mallorquinas, portuguesas, valencianas y bascongadas) de origen oriental: árabe, hebreo, malayo, persa y turco.* Granada: Imprenta de la Lealtad, 1886.

Emeneau, Murray B., and Diether von den Steinen. *Annamese-English Dictionary, with an English-Annamese Index, Based on Work by John Sherry . . . .* Berkeley: Army Specialized Training Program (Univ. of California), 1945.

BIBLIOGRAPHY

Endzelin, Jānis (Ivan M., Johann). *Latyšskie predlogi*. Diss. Dorpat, 1905.

———. *Lettisches Lesebuch, grammatische und metrische Vorbemerkungen, Texte und Glossar*. Heidelberg: C. Winter, 1922.

———. *Slavjano-baltijskie ètjudy*. Xar'kov, 1911.

Engelmann, W. H. *Glossaire des mots espagnols et portugais dérivés de l'arabe*. Leyde: E. J. Brill, 1861.

——— & Dozy, *Id.*, rev. 2d ed. (1869).

Ernault, Émile, ed. *"Le mystère de Sainte Barbe," tragédie bretonne (1557), avec traduction française et dictionnaire étymologique du breton moyen*. Archives de Bretagne, III. Nantes: Société des bibliophiles bretons, 1885-87. (A 2d ed. of the *Glossaire moyen breton* forms Vol. II [Paris: F. Vieweg, 1896] of H. Arbois de Jubainville, *Études grammaticales des langues celtiques*.)

Ernout, Alfred. *Aspects du vocabulaire latin*. Études et commentaires, XVIII. Paris: Klincksieck, 1954.

———. *Le dialecte ombrien: lexique du vocabulaire des "Tables Eugubines" et des inscriptions*. Études et commentaires, XXXVIII. Paris: C. Klincksieck, 1961.

———. *Les éléments dialectaux du vocabulaire latin*. Collection linguistique, III. Paris: La Société de Linguistique, 1909.

——— & Antoine Meillet. *Dictionnaire étymologique de la langue latine; histoire des mots*. Paris: C. Klincksieck, 1932. 2d ed. ("revue, corrigée, et augmentée d'un index"), 1939. 3d ed., 2 vols., 1951. 4th ed., 2 vols., 1959-60.

Falk, Hjalmar S., & Alf Torp. *Etymologisk Ordbog over det norske og det danske Sprog*. 2 vols. Kristiania: H. Aschehoug & Co. (W. Nygaard), 1903-6.

———. *Norwegisch-dänisches etymologisches Wörterbuch*. Auf Grund der Übersetzung von Dr. H[ermann] Davidsen neu bearbeitete deutsche Ausgabe, mit Literaturnachweisen strittiger Etymologien, sowie deutschem und altnordischem Wörterverzeichnis. 2 vols. Sammlung germanischer Elementar– und Handbücher, dir. W. Streitberg, IV: 1. Heidelberg: C. Winter, 1910-11. 2d ed., Oslo: Universitetsforlaget, 1960. [Translation of preceding item.]

———. *Wortschatz der germanischen Spracheinheit* (= A. Fick, *Vergleichendes Wörterbuch*. . ., 4th ed., III). Göttingen: Vandenhoeck & Ruprecht, 1909.

Feist, Sigmund. *Etymologisches Wörterbuch der gotischen Sprache mit Einschluß des sog[enannten] Krimgotischen*. Halle: M. Niemeyer, 1909. 2d ed., entirely recast, 1920-23.

———. *Grundriß der gotischen Etymologie*. Straßburg: K. J. Trübner, 1888.

———. *Vergleichendes Wörterbuch der gotischen Sprache mit Einschluß des Krimgotischen und sonstiger zerstreuter Überreste des Gotischen* [= 3d ed., recast and enlarged, of *Etymologisches Wörterbuch*. . . .]. Leiden: E. J. Brill, 1939.

Fick, August. *Vergleichendes Wörterbuch der indogermanischen Sprachen; ein sprachgeschichtlicher Versuch* [= rev. 2d ed. of *Wörterbuch der indogermanischen Grundsprache*]. 3 vols. in 2. Göttingen: Vandenhoeck & Ruprecht, 1870-71. 3d ed. (rev.) in 4 vols., 1874-76. 4th ed. in 3 vols., rev. by A. Bezzenberger, H. Falk, A. Fick, W. Stokes, and A. Torp, 1890-1909.

———. *Wörterbuch der indogermanischen Grundsprache in ihrem Bestande vor der Völkertrennung*. Preface by T. Benfey. Göttingen, 1868.

108

BIBLIOGRAPHY

Finkenstaedt, Thomas, Ernst Leisi, & Dieter Wolff. *A Chronological English Dictionary, Listing 80000 Words in Order of Their Earliest Known Occurrence.* Heidelberg: C. Winter, 1970. Cf. the companion volume just off the press: Finkenstaedt and Wolff, *Ordered Profusion: Studies in the Dictionaries and the English Lexicon,* Annales Univ. Saraviensis, Reihe: Philos. Fakultät, XIII. Heidelberg: C. Winter, 1973.

Foerster, Wendelin. *Kristian von Troyes. Wörterbuch zu seinen sämtlichen Werken,* unter Mitarbeit von Hermann Breuer. . . . Romanische Bibliothek, XXI. Halle: M. Niemeyer, 1914. (Subsequent editions supervised by Breuer alone: 2d ed., 1933; repr. 3d ed., 1964; new title: *Wörterbuch zu Kr. von Tr.' sämtlichen Werken.*)

Foulet, Lucien. *Glossary of the "First Continuation"* (= Vol. III:2 of William Roach, ed., *The Continuations of the Old French "Perceval" of Chrétien de Troyes.* 3 vols. in 4. Philadelphia: University of Pennsylvania Press, 1949-55).

Fraenkel, Ernst. *Litauisches etymologisches Wörterbuch.* 2 vols. Indogermanische Bibliothek, II: Wörterbücher. Heidelberg: C. Winter, 1962-65.

Franck, Johannes. *Etymologisch woordenboek der nederlandsche taal.* 's-Gravenhage: M. Nijhoff, 1892. 2d ed., rev. by N. van Wijk, with an index of New High German words, 1912-29. *Supplement,* by C. B. van Haeringen, 1936. 3d ed., rev. by N. van Wijk and C. B. van Haeringen, 1949.

———. "Geschichte des Wortes *Hexe,*" reprinted from J. Hansen, *Quellen und Untersuchungen zur Geschichte des Hexenwahns.* . . . Bonn: C. Georgi, 1901.

———. *Mittelniederländische Grammatik, mit Lesestücken und Glossar.* Leipzig: T. O. Weigel, 1883; rev. 2d ed., 1910.

———. *Notgedrungene Beiträge zur Etymologie. Eine Abrechnung mit Prof. Jan te Winkel.* Bonn: F. Cohen, 1893.

Friederici, Georg. *Amerikanistisches Wörterbuch.* Univ. Hamburg, Abhandlungen. . . Auslandskunde, LIII (= B, XXIX). Hamburg: Cram, de Gruyter, 1947.

———. *Hilfswörterbuch für den Amerikanisten. Lehnwörter aus Indianer-sprachen und Erklärungen altertümlicher Ausdrücke, deutsch – spanisch – englisch.* Halle: M. Niemeyer, 1926.

Friedrich, Johannes. *Hethitisches Wörterbuch; kurzgefaßte kritische Sammlung der Deutungen hethitischer Wörter.* Indogermanische Bibliothek, II: Wörterbücher. Heidelberg: C. Winter, 1952-54.

Frings, Theodor. *Romania Germana.* Suppl. 4 to *Teuthonista.* Halle: M. Niemeyer, 1932. 2d ed., rev. by Gertraud Müller, Mitteldeutsche Studien, XIX:1. Halle: Niemeyer, 1966.

Frisk, Hjalmar. *Griechisches etymologisches Wörterbuch.* 3 vols. Heidelberg: C. Winter, 1960-72.

Frommann, G. K.: See under Duden, Konrad.

Gáldi, László, ed. Sámuel Klein, *Dictionarium Valachico-Latinum.* Budapest: Királyi Magyar Egyetemi Nyomda, 1944.

Gallée, Johan Hendrik. *Vorstudien zu einem altniederdeutschen Wörterbuche.* Leiden: E. J. Brill, 1903.

Gamillscheg, Ernst. *Etymologisches Wörterbuch der französischen Sprache.*

BIBLIOGRAPHY

Wortund Sachverzeichnis von Heinrich Kuen. Sammlung romanischer Elementarund Handbücher, dir. W. Meyer-Lübke, III:5. Heidelberg: C. Winter, 19[26]-29; 2d ed., "vollständig neu bearbeitet" (19[66]-69).

――――. *Romania Germanica. Sprach- und Siedlungsgeschichte der Germanen auf dem Boden des alten Römerreichs.* 3 vols. Grundriβ der germanischen Philologie, XI:1-3. Berlin & Leipzig: W. de Gruyter & Co., 1934-36. Rev. 2d ed., Vol. I, Berlin: de Gruyter, 1970.

García de Diego, Vicente. *Contribución al diccionario hispánico etimológico.* Suppl. II to *RFE.* Madrid, 1923. Repr. 1943.

――――. *Diccionario de voces naturales.* Madrid: Aguilar, 1968.

――――. *Diccionario etimológico español e hispánico.* Madrid: S.A.E.T.A. [1954].

――――. *Etimologías españolas.* Biblioteca Cultura e historia. Madrid: Aguilar, 1964.

Geiger, Wilhelm. *An Etymological Glossary of the Sinhalese Language.* Colombo: Royal Asiatic Society, 1941. [A rev. and enlarged ed. of the following item.]

――――. *Etymologie des Singhalesischen.* München: G. Franz, 1898.

Georgacas, Demetrius J. "Grammatische und etymologische Miszellen zum Spät- und Neugriechischen." *Glotta,* XXXI (1951), 199-235.

Gesenius, F. H. W. *Hebräisches und aramäisches Handwörterbuch über das Alte Testament,* 8th ed., rev. F. Mühlau & W. Volck. Leipzig: F. C. W. Vogel, 1878. 9th ed., 1883. 15th ed., rev. F. Buhl, W. M. Müller, O. Weber, H. Zimmer, 1910. 17th ed., 1915. Repr., Berlin: Springer, 1962.

――――. *Lexicon manuale Hebraicum et Chaldaicum in Veteris Testamenti libros.* Lipsiae: F. C. G. Vogel, 1833. [tr. after 3d Germ. ed.]

――――. *Neues hebräisch-deutsches Handwörterbuch über das Alte Testament mit Einschluβ des biblischen Chaldaismus.* Leipzig, 1815.

Gillet, Joseph E. "Corominas' *Diccionario crítico etimológico:* An Appreciation with Suggested Additions." *Hispanic Review,* XXVI (1958), 261-95.

Gombocz, Zoltán, & János Melich. *Magyar etimologiai szótár. Lexicon critico-etymologicum linguae Hungaricae.* 2 vols. (fasc. 1-12). Budapest: Magyar Tudományos Akadémia, 1914-.

Gorjaev, Nikolai. *Ètimologičeskija ob'jasnen'ja naibolee trudnyx i zagadočnyx slov v russkom jazyke. Novyje dopolnen'ja i popravki.* Tiflis, 1905.

――――. *Sravnitel'nyj ètimologičeskij slovar' russkogo jazyka,* 2d ed., Tiflis, 1896. *Dopolnen'ja i popravki* ['Addenda et Corrigenda'], Tiflis, 1901.

Götze, Alfred. See under Kluge, Friedrich.

Graff, E[berhard] G[ottlieb]. *Althochdeutscher Sprachschatz oder Wörterbuch der althochdeutschen Sprache.* 7 vols. Berlin: In Commission der Nikolaischen Buchhandlung, 1834-42. (Companion piece: H. F. Massmann, *Vollständiger alphabetischer Index zu dem...,* Berlin: Nikolaische Buchhandlung, 1846.)

Grandgagnage, Charles. *Dictionnaire étymologique de la langue wallonne.* 2 vols. (I) Liège: F. Oudart, 1845; (II) Liège & Leipzig: Mayer et Flatau, 1880. Bound with a "Supplément," ed. August Scheler: *Glossaire d'anciens mots wallons.* Bruxelles: C. Muquardt, 1880.

――――. *Glossaire des coutumes de Namur.* Bruxelles: F. Gobbaerts, 1874.

Grebe, Paul, rev. *Duden: Etymologie; Herkunftswörterbuch der deutschen*

BIBLIOGRAPHY

Sprache. Mannheim: Bibliographisches Institut, c. 1963 (= *Der große Duden,* VII). Cf. above, under Duden, Konrad.

Grienberger, Th. von. *Untersuchungen zur gotischen Wortkunde.* Akademie Wien: Sitz.-ber., CXLII (1900).

Grierson, George Abraham. *The Pisāca Language in North-western India.* Asiatic Society Monographs, VIII. London: Royal Asiatic Society, 1906. Repr., Delhi: Munshiram Manoharlal [1969].

Grimm, Jakob & Wilhelm. *Deutsches Wörterbuch.* 16 vols. in 45. Leipzig: S. Hirzel, 1854-1960.

Gröber, G. "Lateinische Substrate romanischer Wörter." *ALLG,* I (1884), 204-54; 539-57; II (1885), 100-108, 276-89, 424-44; III (1886), 138-43, 264-75, 507-31; IV (1887), 116-36, 422-54; V (1888), 125-32, 234-42, 453-86; VI (1889), 117-49 and [Supplement], 377-97.

_____. "Sprachquellen und Wortquellen des lateinischen Wörterbuchs." Ibid., I (1884), 35-67.

Haeringen, C. B. van. See under Franck, Johannes.

Haşdeu, Bogdan P[etriceicu]. *Etymologicum magnum Romaniae. Dicţionarul limbei istorice şi poporane a Românilor.* Vols. I-IV. Bucureşti: Academia Românǎ, 1886-98. (I-III: A- to Bǎrbat; IV: Introducerea.)

Haug, M. See under Justi, Ferdinand.

Hauschild, Ernst Innozenz. *Etymologisches Wörterbuch der französischen Sprache nach F. Diez, . . .* Leipzig: J. C. Hinrichs, 1843.

Haust, Jean. *Dictionnaire français-liégeois,* ed. Élisée Legros. Liège: H. Vaillant-Carmanne, 1948.

_____. *Étymologies wallonnes et françaises.* Bibl. de la Fac. de Philos. et Lettres . . . Liège, XXXII. Liège: H. Vaillant-Carmanne, & Paris: É. Champion, 1923.

_____. "Glossaire philologique." In *Régestes de la cité de Liège,* ed. Émile Favion. 4 vols. & Supplement. Liège: Commission communale de l'histoire . . ., 1933-40.

Heinertz, Nils Otto. *Etymologische Studien zum Althochdeutschen.* Skrifter utgivna av Vetenskaps-Societeten i Lund. Lund, 1927.

Hellqvist, Elof. *Svensk etymologisk ordbok.* Lund: C. W. G. Gleerup, 1922; rev. 2d ed., 2 vols., 1935-39. 3d ed., 1948.

Henry, Victor. *Lexique étymologique des termes les plus usuels du breton moderne.* Bibl. bretonne armoricaine, III. Rennes: J. Plihon & L. Hervé, 1900.

Heyse, J. C. A. (1764-1829). *[Allgemeines verdeutschendes und erklärendes] Fremdwörterbuch mit Bezeichnung der Aussprache.* 5th ed., rev. by Gustav Heyse. Hannover: Hahn'sche Hofbuchhandlung, 1873. 9th ed., Leipzig: Fues, 1887. 14th ed., rev. by Carl Böttger, Leipzig, 1903.

Hill, Raymond T. See under Bergin, Thomas G.

Hofmann, Johann B. *Etymologisches Wörterbuch des Griechischen.* 2 vols. in 1. München: R. Oldenbourg, 1949-50.

_____, & Alois Walde. *Lateinisches etymologisches Wörterbuch.* Indogermanische Bibliothek, II: Wörterbücher. 2 vols., plus *Registerband,* comp. Elsbeth Berger. Heidelberg: C. Winter, 1939-65 (= 3d and 4th ed. of A. Walde, *LEW*).

Holthausen, Ferdinand. *Altenglisches etymologisches Wörterbuch.* Germ. Bibl., founded by W. Streitberg (= SGEH, IV:7). Heidelberg: C. Winter, 1934. 2d ed., 1963.

———. *Altfriesisches Wörterbuch*. Germ. Bibl., IV:5. Heidelberg: C. Winter, 1925.

———. *Altsächsisches Wörterbuch*. Niederdeutsche Studien, I. Münster: Böhlau, 1954.

———. *Etymologisches Wörterbuch der englischen Sprache*. Leipzig: Tauchnitz, 1917. 2d ed., "vermehrt und verbessert," 1927. 3d ed., "neubearbeitet und vermehrt," Göttingen: Vandenhoeck & Ruprecht, 1949.

———. *Gotisches etymologisches Wörterbuch, mit Einschluß der Eigennamen und der gotischen Lehnwörter im Romanischen*. Germ. Bibl., IV:8. Heidelberg: C. Winter, 1934.

———. *Vergleichendes und etymologisches Wörterbuch des Altwestnordischen, Altnorwegisch-Isländischen, einschließlich der Lehn- und Fremdwörter sowie der Eigennamen*. Göttingen: Vandenhoeck & Ruprecht, 1948.

Holub, Josef, & Stanislav Lyer. *Stručny etymologický slovník jazyka českého, se zvláštním zřetelem k slovům kulturním a cizím*. Praha: Státní Pedagogické Nakl., 1967.

———. *Stručný slovník etymologický jazyka česko-slovenského*. 2d ed. Praha, 1937.

———. & František Kopečný, *Etimologický slovník jazyka českého*. Praha: Státní Nakl. Učelnik, 1952. [3d ed. of preceding item.]

Horn, Paul. *Grundriß der neupersischen Etymologie*. Sammlung indogermanischer Wörterbücher, IV. Straßburg: Karl J. Trübner, 1893. [Cf. under Heinrich Hübschmann.]

Hubschmid, Johannes. *Alpenwörter romanischen und vorromanischen Ursprungs*. Bern: A. Francke, 1951.

———. *Mediterrane Substrate, mit besonderer Berücksichtigung des Baskischen und der westöstlichen Sprachbeziehungen*. Romania Helvetica, LXX. Bern: A. Francke, 1960.

———. *Praeromanica. Studien zum vorromanischen Wortschatz der Romania mit besonderer Berücksichtigung der frankoprovenzalischen und provenzalischen Mundarten der Westalpen*. Bern: A. Francke, 1949.

———. *Sardische Studien. Das mediterrane Substrat des Sardischen, seine Beziehungen zum Berberischen und Baskischen. . . .* Romania Helvetica, XLI (1953).

———. *Thesaurus Praeromanicus*. Fasc. 1: *Grundlagen für ein weitverbreitetes mediterranes Substrat*, . . .; Fasc. 2: *Probleme der baskischen Lautlehre und baskisch-vorromanische Etymologien*. Bern: A. Francke, 1963-65. [Cf. Y. Malkiel's critique in *Language*, XLVII (1971), 465-87.]

Hübschmann, Heinrich. *Armenische Studien*, I:1: *Grundzüge der armenischen Etymologie*. Leipzig: Breitkopf & Härtel, 1883.

———. *Etymologie und Lautlehre der ossetischen Sprache*. Sammlung indogermanischer Wörterbücher, I. Straßburg: K. J. Trübner, 1887.

———. *Persische Studien*. Straßburg: K. J. Trübner, 1895. [Part I: *Beiträge zu Horn's "Grundriß der neupersischen Etymologie"*; see above, under Horn, Paul.]

Isidorus, Hispalensis episcopus. *Etymologiarum sive Originum libri XX*, ed. W. M. Lindsay. 2 vols. Scriptorum classicorum bibliotheca oxoniensis. Oxford: Clarendon Press, 1911.

BIBLIOGRAPHY

Jaberg, Karl (& Jakob Jud). *Index zum "Sprach- und Sachatlas Italiens und der Südschweiz". Ein propädeutisches etymologisches Wörterbuch der italienischen Mundarten*. Bern: Stämpfli & Co., 1960.

Jakobsen, Jakob (†1918). *An Etymological Dictionary of the Norn Language in Shetland*, ed. Anna Horsböl. 2 vols. London: D. Nutt (A. G. Berry), & Copenhagen: V. Prior, 1928-32.

———. *Etymologisk ordbog over det norrφne sprog på Shetland*, ed. Marie Mikkelsen. 2 vols. Kφbenhavn: V. Prior, 1921.

———. *The Place-Names in Shetland*, tr. Anna Horsböl [from Danish original, 1901]. London: D. Nutt, & Copenhagen: V. Prior, 1936. (Appendix: "Old Stream Names and Names of Fishing Grounds in Shetland, Iceland, the Faeroes and Orkneys," Dan. orig. 1922.)

Jarník, Johann Urban. *Glossaire des chansons populaires roumaines de Transylvanie*. Prague: Imprimerie E. Grégr ("imprimé aux frais de l'Académie Roumaine"), 1885.

———. *Versuch eines Etymologikons der slowenischen Mundart im Innern Österreichs*. Klagenfurt, 1832. See also under Diez, Friedrich.

Jessen, E[dvin]. *Dansk Etymologisk Ordbog*. Kφbenhavn: Gyldendal, 1893.

Jóhannesson, Alexander. *Isländisches etymologisches Wörterbuch*. Bern: A. Francke, 1956.

Jokl, Norbert. *Linguistisch-kulturhistorische Untersuchungen aus dem Bereiche des Albanesischen*. Berlin & Leipzig: W. de Gruyter & Co., 1923.

———. *Studien zur albanesischen Etymologie und Wortbildung*. Akademie Wien, Sitz.-ber., CLXVIII:1 (1911).

Justi, Ferdinand. *Handbuch der Zendsprache. Altbactrisches Wörterbuch. Grammatik. Chrestomathie*. Leipzig: 1864. Repr.: Wiesbaden: M. Sändig, 1969. (Cf. M. Haug, *Über den gegenwärtigen Stand der Zendphilologie, mit besonderer Rücksicht auf F. Justi's "Altbactrisches Wörterbuch"; ein Beitrag zur Erklärung Zendawesta*. Stuttgart: C. Grüninger, 1868.)

———. *Iranisches Namenbuch*. Marburg: N. G. Elwert, 1895.

Kahane, Henry & Renée, and Andreas Tietze. *The Lingua Franca in the Levant. Turkish Nautical Terms of Italian and Greek Origin*. Urbana: University of Illinois Press, 1958.

Kelkar, A. "The Scope of a Historical Dictionary." In: *Studies in Historical Sanskrit Lexicography*. Poona: Deccan College, 1973, pp. 57-69.

Keller, Hans Erich. See under Wartburg, Walther von.

Keniston, Hayward, ed. *Fuero de Guadalajara (1219)*. Elliott Monographs ..., XVI. Princeton: University Press, and Paris: Les Presses universitaires de France, 1924.

Klein, Ernest. *A Comprehensive Etymological Dictionary of the English Language, Dealing with the Origin of Words and Their Sense Development. . . .* 2 vols. Amsterdam, London, & New York: Elsevier, 1966-67.

Klein, Sámuel (1745-1806). See under Gáldi, László.

Kluge, Friedrich. *An Etymological Dictionary of the German Language*, tr. John Francis Davis (from the 4th German ed.). London: G. Bell & Sons, 1891.

———. *Etymologisches Wörterbuch der deutschen Sprache*. 1st and 2d ed., Straβburg: K. J. Trübner, 1883. 3d ed., 1884. Rev. 4th ed., 1889. Rev. 5th ed., 1894. Rev. 6th ed., 1899; reprint, 1905. Rev. 7th ed., 1910. Rev. 8th ed., 19[14-]15; includes "Verzeichnis der zu Altersbestimmungen zugezogenen deutschen Wörterbücher"); 9th ed. ("durchgesehen"), Berlin & Leipzig: W. de Gruyter & Co., 1921. 10th ed., 1924. 11th ed., rev. by Alfred Götze and Wolfgang Krause, 19[30]-34. 12th and 13th ed., 1943. 14th, 15th, and 16th ed., completely revised by Alfred Götze, ed. Hans Krahe, Berlin: W. de Gruyter, 1951. 17th ed., rev. by Walther Mitzka and Alfred Schirmer, 1957. 18th ed., rev. by W. Mitzka, 1960. 19th ed., 1963. 20th ed., 1967. Cf. Vincent Franz Janssen, *Gesamtindex zu Kluges EWDS*, Straβburg: K. J. Trübner, 1890.

———, & Frederick Lutz. *English Etymology; a Select Glossary Serving as an Introduction to the History of the English Language*. Boston: D. C. Heath (and Straβburg: K. J. Trübner), 1898. Reissued in London, 1899.

Koenig, Eduard. *Hebräisches und aramäisches Wörterbuch zum Alten Testament*. Leipzig: Dieterich, 1910; 2d and 3d ed., 1922. 4th and 5th ed., 1931.

Körting, Gustav. *Etymologisches Wörterbuch der französischen Sprache*. Paderborn: F. Schöningh, 1908.

———. *Lateinisch-romanisches Wörterbuch. Etymologisches Wörterbuch der romanischen Hauptsprachen*. Paderborn: F. Schöningh, 1891. Rev. 2d ed., 1901. Rev. 3d ed., 1907. Repr. by G. E. Stechert, New York, 1923.

———. *Taschenwörterbuch der deutschen Sprache*, I: *Etymologisches Lehn- und Fremdwörterbuch*. Berlin-Schöneberg: G. Langenscheidt, 1910.

Kraelitz-Greifenhorst, Friedrich Edler von. *Corollarien zu F. Miklosich, "Die türkischen Elemente in den südost- und osteuropäischen Sprachen (griechisch, albanisch, rumänisch, bulgarisch, servisch, kleinrussisch, groβrussisch, polnisch)."* Akad. Wien., Sitz.-ber. CLXVI:4 (1911). Cf. under Miklosich, Franz.

Krause, Wolfgang. See under Kluge, Friedrich.

Kriaras, Emmanouēl. Λεξικὸ τῆς μεσαιωνικῆς ἑλληνικῆς δημώδους γραμματείας, *1100-1669*. 2 vols. so far; to continue. Thessalonike: R[oyal] Hellenic Research Foundation, © 1968-.

Kronasser, Heinz. *Etymologie der hethitischen Sprache:* I. *Zur Schreibung und Lautung des Hethitischen;* II. *Wortbildung des Hethitischen*. 6 fascicles in 5. Wiesbaden: Otto Harrassowitz, 1962-66.

Kuen, Heinrich. See under Gamillscheg, Ernst.

Kulkarni, K. P. *Marathi Etymological Dictionary*. Poona, 1964.

Lafon, René. *Les formes simples du verbe basque dans les principaux textes du XVIᵉ siècle; structure du système et emploi des formes*. Thèse principale, Paris. Bordeaux: Delmas, 1943.

———. *Le système des formes verbales à auxiliaire dans les principaux textes basques du XVIᵉ siècle*. Thèse complémentaire, Paris. Bordeaux: Delmas, 1943.

Lapa, Manuel Rodrigues, ed. *Cantigas d'escarnho e de mal dizer dos cancioneiros medievais galego-portugueses*. Rev. 2d ed. Colección Filolóxica. N. pl. [printed in Coimbra]: Editorial Galaxia, 1970. Bound with: *Vocabulário galego-português extraído da edição crítica das . . .* [separate pagination].

Laroche, Emmanuel. *Dictionnaire de la langue louvite*. Bibl. archéol. et hist. de l'Institut Français d'Archéologie d'Istanbul. Paris: Librairie Adrien-Maisonneuve, 1951.

Lebrun, Louis, & Joseph Toisoul. *Dictionnaire étymologique de la langue*

française, basé sur le groupement des mots en tableaux synoptiques, ...
Paris: F. Nathan, 1925. New ed., Paris, 1937.

Lenz, Rodolfo. *Diccionario etimológico de las voces chilenas derivadas de lenguas indígenas americanas.* 2 vols. Supplement to *Anales de la Universidad de Chile.* Santiago de Chile: Imprenta Cervantes, 1905-10.

Lévrier, Gabriel. *Dictionnaire étymologique du patois poitevin.* Niort, 1867.

Levy, Emil [& Carl Appel]. *Provenzalisches Supplement-wörterbuch; Berichtigungen und Ergänzungen zu Raynouards "Lexique roman."* 8 vols. Leipzig: O. R. Reisland, 1894-1924.

Lewy, Heinrich. *Die semitischen Fremdwörter im Griechischen.* Berlin: R. Gaertner, 1895.

Lidén, Evald. *Armenische Studien.* GHÅ, XII:2 (1906).

_____. *Ordstudier.* Meyerbergs Arkiv för svensk ordforskning, I. Göteborg, 1937.

_____. *Studien zur altindischen und vergleichenden Sprachgeschichte.* Skrifter utg. af K. Human. Vetenskapssamfundet, VI:1. Uppsala, 1897.

_____. *Studien zur tocharischen Sprachgeschichte,* I. GHÅ, XXII:3. Göteborg, 1916.

_____. *Vermischtes zur Wortkunde und Grammatik.* Språkvetenskapliga Sällskapets i Uppsala Förhandlingar. Uppsala, 1891-94.

Littmann, Enno (†1958). "Anhang: Die in diesem Namenbuche vorkommenden abessinischen, arabischen, aramäischen, kanaanäischen und persischen Namen" (1922), see under Preisigke, Friedrich: *Namenbuch.* . . .

_____. *Morgenländische Wörter im Deutschen.* Berlin: K. Curtius, 1920. 2d ed. ("vermehrt und verbessert," "mit einem Anhang über die amerikanischen Wörter"). Tübingen: J. C. B. Mohr, 1924.

_____ & Maria Höfner. *Wörterbuch der Tigré-Sprache: Tigré – Deutsch – Englisch.* Wiesbaden: F. Steiner, 1962.

Littré, Émile. *Dictionnaire de la langue française contenant* . . . *la nomenclature* . . . *la grammaire* . . . *la signification des mots* . . . *la partie historique* . . . *l'étymologie.* 4 vols., issued in 30 parts. Paris: Hachette et Cie, 1863-72. Later editions 1875, 1882; in 7 vols.: Paris: [Vols. I-IV] J. J. Pauvert, [Vols. V-VII] Gallimard, 1956-58.

_____. *Supplément renfermant un grand nombre de termes d'art, de science, d'agriculture, etc. et de néologismes de tous genres* . . . [includes M. Devic's dictionary of Oriental words]. Paris-Londres: Hachette, 1877, 1881, 1883.

_____. *Abrégé, avec un Supplément d'histoire et de géographie* par A. Beaujean. 5th ed., Paris: Hachette, 1881. New ed. ("entièrement refondue"), 1891.

_____, & Charles Robin. *Dictionnaire de médecine, de chirurgie, de pharmacie.* . . . Paris & Londres: J.-B. Baillière, 1878; 15th ed. (1884); 21st ed., rev. by A. Gilbert, 1908.

Lokotsch, Karl. *Etymologisches Wörterbuch der amerikanischen (indianischen) Wörter im Deutschen, mit steter Berücksichtigung der englischen, spanischen und französischen Formen.* Germanische Bibliothek, IV:6. Heidelberg: C. Winter, 1926.

_____. *Etymologisches Wörterbuch der europäischen (germanischen, romanischen und slawischen) Wörter orientalischen Ursprungs.* Heidelberg: C. Winter, 1927.

Lommatzsch, Erhard. See under Tobler, Adolf.

115

Löpelmann, Martin, *Etymologisches Wörterbuch der baskischen Sprache. Dialekte von Labourd, Nieder-Navarra und La Soule.* 2 vols. Berlin: W. de Gruyter, 1968.

Lutz, Frederick. See under Kluge, Friedrich.

Macbain, Alexander (†1907). *An Etymological Dictionary of the Gaelic Language.* 7th ed. (rev. by Calum MacPharlain). Inverness & Stirling: E. Mackay, 1911. [The author's "Further Gaelic Words and Etymologies" has been incorporated.]

——. "Etymology of the Principal Gaelic National Names, Personal Names and Surnames, . . ." Repr. from *EDGL,* above. Stirling: E. Mackay, 1911.

——. *Place-Names, Highlands, and Islands of Scotland,* ed. William J. Watson. Stirling: J. Mackay, 1922.

Machek, Václav. *Česká a slovenská jména rostlin.* Praha: Nakl. Československé Akademie Věd, 1954.

——. *Etimologický slovník jazyka českého a slovenského.* Praha: Nakl. Československé Akademie Věd, 1957. Rev. 2d ed., with shortened title, 1968.

——. *Recherches dans le domaine du lexique balto-slave.* Spisy Filosofické Fakulty Masarykovy Universitety, XXXVII. Brno: 1934.

Mahn, Karl August Friedrich. *Etymologische Untersuchungen auf dem Gebiet der romanischen Sprachen.* Specimens 1-24. Berlin: W. Dümmler, 1863-76.

Malkiel, Yakov: See under Hubschmid, Johannes.

Mann, Stuart Edward. *An Armenian Historical Grammar in Latin Characters: Morphology, Etymology, Old Texts.* London: Luzac, 1968.

——. *An English-Albanian Dictionary.* Cambridge: University Press, 1957.

——. *An Historical Albanian-English Dictionary.* London, New York: Longmans, Green, 1948. [There exists a Brno, 1938 ed. under the title: *An Historical Albanian and English Dictionary (1496-1938)*].

——. *A Short Albanian Grammar with Vocabularies and Selected Passages for Reading.* London: D. Nutt, 1932.

Marden, C. Carroll, ed. *"Libro de Apolonio," an Old Spanish Poem.* 2 vols. Elliott Monographs . . ., VI, XI-XII. Baltimore: The Johns Hopkins Press, & Paris: É. Champion, 1917-22.

——, ed. *"Poema de Fernán Gonçález"; texto crítico, con introducción, notas y glosario.* Baltimore: The Johns Hopkins Press, 1904.

Marouzeau, Jules. *Lexique de la terminologie linguistique.* Paris: P. Geuthner, 1933. 2d ed. ("augmentée et mise au jour"), 1943 [Subtitle: "Français, allemand, anglais"]. 3d ed., 1951. Tr. by N. D. Andreev: *Slovar' lingvističeskoj terminologii,* Preface by V. A. Zvegincev, Moskva, 1960.

Marzano, Giovanni Battista. *Dizionario etimologico del dialetto calabrese.* Laureana di Borrello: Il Progresso, 1928 [posthumous].

Marzell, Heinrich, & Wilhelm Wissmann. *Wörterbuch der deutschen Pflanzennamen.* 2 vols. Leipzig: S. Hirzel, 1943-58.

Matthes, H. Ch.: see under Holthausen, Ferdinand.

Mayrhofer, Manfred. *Handbuch des Pāli, mit Texten und Glossar. Eine Einführung in das sprachwissenschaftliche Studium des Mittelindischen.* 2 vols. I: *Grammatik,* II: *Texte und Glossar.* Heidelberg: C. Winter, 1951.

——. *Kurzgefaßtes etymologisches Wörterbuch des Altindischen. A Concise*

Etymological Sanskrit Dictionary, 2 vols., I: *A-Th,* II: *D-M.* (To continue) Indogermanische Bibliothek, II: Wörterbücher. Heidelberg: C. Winter, 1956-63.

Meillet, Antoine. *Études sur l'étymologie et le vocabulaire du vieux slave.* Bibl. de l'École des Hautes Études, CXXXIX:1-2. Paris, 1902-5. See also under Bloch, Oscar.

Melich, János: See under Gombocz, Zoltán.

Ménage, Gilles. *Les origines de la langue françoise.* Paris: Augustin Courbé, 1650. Rev. 2d ed., 1694.

Menéndez Pidal, Ramón, ed. *Cantar de Mio Cid: texto, gramática y vocabulario.* 3 vols.; II: *Vocabulario,* Madrid, 1908. Included in *Obras (completas),* Vol. IV, Madrid, 1945; pp. 423-904.

———. *Manual (elemental) de gramática histórica española.* Madrid: V. Suárez, 1904. Rev. 2d ed., 1905. Rev. 3d ed., 1909. Rev. 4th ed., 1918. Rev. 5th ed., 1925; repr. 1929. Rev. 6th ed., 1941; numerous reprints.

———. *Orígenes del español; estudio lingüístico de la Península Ibérica hasta el siglo XI,* Madrid: Suppl. I to *RFE,* 1928. Rev. 2d ed., 1929. Rev. 3d ed., 1950 (= *Obras:* Espasa-Calpe, VIII). The 4th ed. and the 5th ed. (1964) are mere reprints of the 3d.

Menges, K. H. *The Oriental Elements in the Vocabulary of the Oldest Russian Epos.* Suppl. 7 to *Word.* New York, 1951.

Metzenthin, Esther Marie. *Die Länder- und Völkernamen im altisländischen Schrifttum.* Bryn Mawr, Pa., 1941. [Based on author's Bryn Mawr dissertation, 1935.]

Meyer, Gustav. *Albanesische Studien,* I-III. Akad. Wien, Sitz.-ber. CIV, CVII, CXXV (1883-96). [Includes "Die albanesischen Zahlwörter."]

———. *Etymologisches Wörterbuch der albanesischen Sprache.* Sammlung indogermanischer Wörterbücher, III. Straßburg: K. J. Trübner, 1891.

———. *Neugriechische Studien,* I-IV. Akad. Wien, Sitz.-ber. CXXX:4-5, CXXXII:3, 6 (1894-95). [Includes: "Die slavischen, albanesischen und rumänischen Lehnworte im Neugriechischen"; "Die lateinischen Lehnworte im Neugriechischen"; "Die romanischen Lehnworte im Neugriechischen."]

———. *Türkische Studien,* I: *Die griechischen und romanischen Bestandteile im Wortschatz des Osmanisch-Türkischen.* Akad. Wien, Sitz.-ber., CXXVIII:1 (1893).

Meyer-Lübke, Wilhelm. *Romanische Namenstudien.* 2 vols. Akad. Wien, Sitz.-ber., CXLIX:2 (1909) and CLXXXIV:4 (1917).

———. *Romanisches etymologisches Wörterbuch.* Sammlung romanischer Elementar- und Handbücher, III:3. Heidelberg: C. Winter, 1911 [-20]. Repr. in the early 'twenties [= 2d ed.]. Rev. ("vollständig neubearbeitet") 3d ed., 1930-35. See also under Nascentes, Anténor.

Michaëlis (de Vasconcelos), Carolina. "Contribuïções para o futuro dicionário etimológico. . . ." *RL,* XI (1908), 1-62. "Mestre Giraldo e os seus tratados. . ., II. Estudos etimológicos." Ibid., XIII (1910), 223-432.

———. "Studien zur romanischen Wortdeutung." In *In memoria di Napoleone Caix e Ugo Angelo Canello: Miscellanea di filologia e linguistica,* pp. 113-66. Firenze: Succ. Le Monnier, 1886.

Cf. G. Moldenhauer's bibliography of her writings ushering in the *Miscelânea*

117

de estudos em honra de D. C. M. de V., Coimbra: Imprensa da Universidade, 1933.

Migliorini, Bruno. *Dal nome proprio al nome comune; studi semantici sul mutamento dei nomi propri di persona in nomi comuni negl' idiomi romanzi.* Bibl. dell' "Archivum Romanicum," II:13. Genève: L. S. Olschki, 1927. Rev. 2d ed. ("ristampa fotografica . . . con un supplemento"), 1968.

_____, with Aldo Duro. *Prontuario etimologico della lingua italiana.* Torino: G. B. Paravia, 1950. 2d ed., 1953. 3d ed., 1958.

Mikkola, J. J. *Baltisches und Slavisches.* Finska Vetenskap Soc., Förhandlingar, XLV. Helsinki, 1903.

_____. *Berührungen zwischen den westfinnischen und den slawischen Sprachen.* Mémoires de la Société Finno-Ougrienne, VIII. Helsinki, 1894.

Miklosich, Franz. *Dictionnaire abrégé des six langues slaves (russe, vieux-slave, bulgare, serbe, tchèque et polonaise)* . . . . St. Peterburg – Moskva: M. O. Wolff, 1885.

_____. *Etymologisches Wörterbuch der slawischen Sprachen.* Wien: W. Braumüller, 1886.

_____. *Die Fremdwörter in den slawischen Sprachen.* Akad. Wien, Denkschrift XV (1867).

_____. *Die türkischen Elemente in den südost- und osteuropäischen Sprachen . . .,* I-II (with two Supplements). Akad. Wien, Denkschrift XXXIV (1884), XXXV (1885), XXXVIII (1890). Cf. under Kraelitz-Greifenhorst, Friedrich.

Mitterand, Henri. See under Dauzat, Albert.

Mitzka, Walther. See under Kluge, Friedrich.

Mladenov, Stefan. *Ètimologičeski i pravopisen rečnik na bŭlgarskija knižoven ezik.* Sofia: X. G. Danov, 1941.

Möller, Hermann. "Expansion of *Indoeuropeisk-semitisk sammenlignende glossarium."* In *Festskrift Kjøbenhavn Universitet.* 1909.

_____. *Vergleichendes indogermanisch-semitisches Wörterbuch.* Göttingen: Vandenhoeck & Ruprecht, 1911.

Monlau, Pedro Felipe. *Diccionario etimológico de la lengua castellana, precedido de unos rudimentos de etimología.* Madrid: M. Rivadeneyra, 1856. Rev. 2d ed., with a Preface by José Monlau, 1881. With a Preface by A. Herrero Mayor, Buenos Aires: El Ateneo, 1941.

Moravcsik, Gyula. *Byzantino-Turcica.* 2 vols. Budapest, 1942-43; rev. 2d ed., Berlin: Akademie Verlag, 1958 (= Berliner Byzantinische Arbeiten, X-XI). [Includes: "Sprachreste der Türkvölker in den byzantinischen Quellen."]

Morgenstierne, Georg. *An Etymological Vocabulary of Pashto.* Skrifter utgitt av Det Norske Videnskaps Akademie, II: Hist.-Filos. Kl., 1927:3.

_____. *Etymological Vocabulary of the Shugni Group.* Beiträge zur Iranistik. Wiesbaden: Dr. Ludwig Reichert Verlag, 1973.

Müller, Eduard. *Etymologisches Wörterbuch der englischen Sprache.* 2 parts in 1 vol. Coethen: P. Schettler, 1865-67.

Muller, Frederik (Jzn.). *Altitalisches Wörterbuch.* Göttingen: Vandenhoeck & Ruprecht, 1926.

_____. *De veterum, imprimis Romanorum, studiis etymologicis,* I. Diss. Traiecti ad Rhenum [= Utrecht], 1910.

19999BIBLIOGRAPHY

Nascentes, Anténor. *Dicionário etimológico da língua portuguesa.* Preface by W. Meyer-Lübke. Rio de Janeiro, 1932.

_____. *Dicionário etimológico resumido.* Rio de Janeiro: Instituto Nacional do Livro, 1966.

_____. *Tesouro da fraseologia brasileira.* Rio de Janeiro & São Paulo: Freitas Bastos, 1945. 2d ed., 1966.

Nash, Rose. *Multilingual Lexicon of Linguistics and Philology: English, Russian, German, French.* Miami Linguistics Series, III. Coral Gables: University of Miami Press, 1968.

Navarro Viola, Alberto. *Juicio crítico del "Diccionario filológico comparado de la lengua castellana" [de Calandrelli].* Buenos Aires, 1884. [Calandrelli's work contrasted with Barcia's.]

Nebrixa, (E.) A. de (†1522). *Dictionarium . . . imo quadruplex eiusdem antiqui dictionarij supplementum.* Rev. ed. Madrid: A. Marín & G. Ramírez, 1751. Rev. by López de Rubiños, Madrid: A. Marino, 1754. Rev. by Eugenio Zeballos, Madrid: J. Ibarra, 1771.

_____. *Vocabulario español-latino.* Salamanca, [1495?]. Facsimile ed., Madrid: R. Academia Española, 1951.

Niedermann, Max. *Balto-Slavica.* Genève: Librairie Droz, 1956.

_____. *Contributions à la critique et à l'explication des gloses latines.* Neuchâtel, 1905.

_____. *Essais d'étymologie et de critique verbale latines.* Neuchâtel: Attinger, 1918.

_____, with Franz Brender, A. Salys, & Alfred Senn.*Wörterbuch der litauischen Schriftsprache.* 5 vols. Heidelberg: C. Winter, 1926/32-1968.

Nielsen, Konrad. *Lappisk ordbok.* 5 vols. Oslo: H. Aschehoug & Co., & Cambridge, Mass.: Harvard University Press, 1932-62.

"Nizier du Puitspelu" [pseud. = Clair Tisseur]. *Dictionnaire étymologique du patois lyonnais.* Lyon: H. Georg, 1889-90.

Nunn, Marshall E. *A List of Related Spanish-English Words.* University, Ala.: Bureau of Business Research, University of Alabama, 1944.

_____, & Herbert E. Van Scoy. *Glossary of Related Spanish-English Words.* University of Alabama Studies, V. University, Ala.: University of Alabama Press, 1949.

Odhner, Einar. *Vad betyder orden? Etymologisk ordlista.* Stockholm: Liber, 1952. Rev. 2d ed., titled *Etymologisk ordlista; våra ords ursprung och betydelse,* 1967.

_____. *Växternas nam, deras betydelse och ursprung.* Rev. 2d ed. Stockholm: Liber, 1965 (© 1963).

Olivieri, Dante. *I cognomi della Venezia Euganea; saggio di uno studio storico etimologico,* 1923. [Forms, with P. Aebischer's *Sur l'origine et la formation des noms de famille . . .,* a volume titled *Onomastica.*]

_____. *Dizionario di toponomastica lombarda; nomi di comuni, frazioni, casali, monti, corsi d'acqua. . . .* Milano: Meneghina, 1931. Rev. 2d ed., Milano: Ceschina, 1961.

_____. *Dizionario di toponomastica piemontese.* Brescia: Paideia, 1965.

_____. *Dizionario etimologico italiano, concordato coi dialetti, le lingue straniere e la topo-onomastica.* Milano: Ceschina [1953]. Rev. 2d ed., 1961.

——. *Saggio di una illustrazione generale della toponomastica veneta.* Città di Castello: S. Lapi, 1914-15. Rev. 2d ed., under the new title *Toponomastica veneta (Civiltà veneziana),* Venezia & Roma: Istituto per la collaborazione culturale, 1961.

Onions, C. T., with the assistance of G. W. S. Friedrichsen & R. W. Burchfield. *The Oxford Dictionary of English Etymology.* Oxford: Clarendon Press, 1966.

Osthoff, Hermann. *Etymologische Parerga.* Leipzig, 1901.

(Palander-) Suolahti, Hugo. *Die althochdeutschen Tiernamen,* I: *Die Namen der Säugetiere.* Diss. Helsinki. Darmstadt: G. Otto, 1899.

——. *Die deutschen Vogelnamen; eine wortgeschichtliche Untersuchung.* Straβburg: K. J. Trübner, 1909.

Palmer, Philip M. *Der Einfluβ der Neuen Welt auf den deutschen Wortschatz.* Germanische Bibliothek, II:35. Heidelberg: C. Winter, 1933.

——. *Neuweltwörter im Deutschen.* Germanische Bibliothek, II:42. Heidelberg: C. Winter, 1939.

Papahagi, Tache (Pericle). *Dicţionarul dialectului aromîn, general şi etimologic.* Bucureşti: Editura Academiei Romîne, 1963.

——. *Parallele Ausdrücke und Redensarten im Rumänischen, Albanesischen, Neugriechischen und Bulgarischen.* Diss. Leipzig, 1908.

Pape, Wilhelm. *Etymologisches Wörterbuch der griechischen Sprache, zur Übersicht der Wortbildung nach den Endsilben geordnet.* Berlin: F. Dümmler, 1836.

—— *Wörterbuch der griechischen Eigennamen, nebst einer Übersicht über die Bildung der Personennamen.* Braunschweig: F. Vieweg, 1842. Rev. 2d ed., 1850. 3d ed., rev. by G. E. Benseler, 2 vols., Braunschweig, 1863-70.

Partridge, Eric. *Origins. A Short Etymological Dictionary of Modern English.* London & New York: Macmillan, 1958. Rev. 2d ed. (1959); 3d ed. (1961); 4th ed. ("with numerous revisions and some substantial additions"), London: Routledge & K. Paul, 1966.

Partridge, H. B.: See under Pokorny, Julius.

Paul, Hermann. *Deutsches Wörterbuch.* Halle: M. Niemeyer, 1897. Rev. 2d ed., 1908. 3d ed., 1921. 4th ed., rev. by Karl Euling, Halle, 1935. 5th ed., rev. by Werner Betz ("völlig neubearbeitet und erweitert"), Tübingen [West Germany]: M. Niemeyer, 1957-66. 7th ed., rev. by A. Schirmer, Halle [East Germany]: M. Niemeyer, 1960.

Pellegrini, Giovanni Battista. *Gli arabismi nelle lingue neolatine; con speciale riguardo all'Italia.* 2 vols. Brescia: Paideia, 1972.

Petersson, Herbert. *Arische und armenische Studien.* LUÅ, N.F. (I), XVI:3. (1920).

——. *Baltisches und Slawisches.* LUÅ, XII:2 (1916).

——. *Baltische und slawische Wortstudien.* LUÅ, XIV:31 (1918).

——. *Zur slawischen und vergleichenden Wortschöpfung.* LUÅ, XI:5 (1915).

——. *Vergleichende slawische Wortstudien.* LUÅ, XVIII:21. Lund, 1922.

——. *Vermische Beiträge zur Wortforschung.* Filol. Fören. Lund, IV. Lund, 1915.

Pianigiani, Ottorino. *Vocabolario etimologico della lingua italiana.* Preface by F. L. Pullè. Roma, 1907. Rev. 2d ed., 2 vols., Milano: Casa Editrice Sonzogno,

1937, 1942. *Aggiunte, correzioni e variazioni al VEdLI*, Firenze: E. Ariani, 1926.

Pinloche, Auguste, & Theodor Matthias. *Etymologisches Wörterbuch der deutschen Sprache, enthaltend: ein Bilder-Wörterbuch.* . . . Paris: Larousse, 1922. Rev. 2d ed., Wien, 1932.

Plate, Rudolf. *Etymologisches Wörterbuch* [binder's title: *Lexikon*] *der französischen Sprache.* Berlin & Bonn: F. Dümmler, 1931. [Cf. E. Gamillscheg, *ZFSL*, LV (1930), 117-19; see also p. 128.]

_____. *Französische Wortkunde auf sprach- und kulturgeschichtlicher Grundlage.* 2d ed., rev. by Hans-Wilhelm Klein. München: M. Hueber, 1955.

Pokorny, Julius. *Indogermanisches etymologisches Wörterbuch.* 2 vols. Bern & München: A. Francke, 19[48]-59-1969. [Vol. II is a *Registerband*, which should have been credited on the title page to its compiler, Harry B. Partridge.] See also under Walde, Alois.

Prati, Angelino. *Dialettismi nell'italiano.* Pisa: Goliardica, 1954.

_____. *Etimologie venete*, ed. Gianfranco Folena & Giambattista Pellegrini. Civiltà veneziana: Dizionari dialettali, IV. Venezia & Roma: Istituto per la collaborazione culturale, 1968.

_____. *Prontuario di parole moderne.* Roma: Ateneo, 1952.

_____. *Ricerche di toponomastica.* Rovereto, 1910.

_____. *Voci di gerganti, vagabondi e malviventi, studiate nell'origine e nella storia.* Suppl. II (1940) to *L'Italia dialettale.*

_____.*Vocabolario etimologico italiano.* Milano: Garzanti, 1951.

Preisigke, Friedrich. *Namenbuch, enthaltend alle griechischen, lateinischen, ägyptischen, hebräischen, arabischen und sonstigen semitischen und nichtsemitischen Menschennamen, soweit sie in griechischen Urkunden . . . Ägyptens sich vorfinden.* Heidelberg: Selbstverlag, 1922. Cf. Daniele Foraboschi, *"Onomasticon Alternum Papyrologicum"; Supplemento al "Namenbuch".* Milano: Istituto Editoriale Cisalpino, 1967.

Prellwitz, Walther. *Etymologisches Wörterbuch der griechischen Sprache, mit besonderer Berücksichtigung des Neuhochdeutschen und einem deutschen Wörterverzeichnis.* Göttingen: Vandenhoeck & Ruprecht, 1892. Rev. 2d ed. (1905).

Preobraženskij, Antonin. *Ètimologičeskij slovar' russkogo jazyka.* 14 fasc.: *A-Su.* Moskva: G. Lissner & D. Sovko (printers), 1910-18. Cf. R. Jakobson, *Word,* VII (1951), 187f.

Puşcariu, Sextil. *Etymologisches Wörterbuch der rumänischen Sprache,* I: *Lateinisches Element, mit Berücksichtigung aller romanischen Sprachen.* Sammlung romanischer Elementarbücher, III:1. Heidelberg: C. Winter, 1905.

Quemada, Bernard. *Les dictionnaires du français moderne, 1539-1863: Étude sur leur histoire, leurs types et leurs méthodes.* Études lexicologiques, I. Paris, Bruxelles, Montréal: Didier, 1967.

Qvigstad, Just Knud. *De lappiske stedsnavn i Troms fylke.* Oslo: H. Aschehoug, & Cambridge: Harvard University Press, 1935.

_____. *Nordische Lehnwörter im Lappischen.* Oslo: Norse Videnskaps Akademie, Forhandlinger, 1893.

Ramstedt, R. J. *Studies in Korean Etymologies.* Mémoires de la Société Finno-Ougrienne, XCV. Helsinki, 1949.

Raynouard, François (†1836). *Lexique roman; ou, Dictionnaire de la langue des*

BIBLIOGRAPHY

troubadours comparée avec les autres langues de l'Europe latine. 6 vols. Paris: Silvestre, 1844. [Vols. II-V contain the core.]

Reichardt, Konstantin. See under Walde, Alois, and Julius Pokonry.

Rheinfelder, Hans. Kultsprache und Profansprache in den romanischen Ländern. Sprachgeschichtliche Studien. . . . Bibl. dell' "Archivum Romanicum", II: 18. Genève: L. S. Olschki, 1933.

Rey-Debove, Josette. Étude linguistique et sémiotique des dictionnaires français contemporains. Approaches to Semiotics, dir. Thomas A. Sebeok, XIII. The Hague & Paris: Mouton, 1971.

Richardson, Henry Brush. An Etymological Vocabulary to the "Libro de Buen Amor" of Juan Ruiz. . . . Yale Romanic Studies, II. New Haven: Yale University Press, 1930.

Robert, Paul. Dictionnaire alphabétique et analogique de la langue française. Les mots et les associations d'idées. Paris: Société du Nouveau Littré, 1965-.

Rohlfs, Gerhard. Dizionario dialettale delle tre Calabrie, con note etimologiche e un'introduzione sulla storia dei dialetti calabresi. . . . Two parts in 3 vols. (I-II: Calabrese-Italiano: III: Italiano-Calabrese). Halle: M. Niemeyer, & Milano: U. Hoepli, 1932-39.

———. Etymologisches Wörterbuch der unteritalienischen Gräzität. Halle: M. Niemeyer, 1930.

———. Lexicon Graecanicum Italiae Inferioris. Etymologisches Wörterbuch der unteritalienischen Gräzität. Rev. 2d ed. ("erweitert und völlig neubearbeitet") of preceding item. Tübingen: M. Niemeyer, 1964. Cf. the review article by H. and R. Kahane ("Greek in Southern Italy") in RPh, XX:4 (1967), 404-38.

Roques, Mario, comp. Recueil général des lexiques français du moyen âge (XIIe-XVe siècle). 2 vols. Bibl. de l'École des Hautes Études, CCLXIV, CCLXIX. Paris: H. Champion, 1936-38. (Lexiques alphabétiques: Latin-français).

Rosal, Francisco del. Origen y etimología de todos los vocablos originales de la lengua castellana; unpubl. MS, 1601. (For entries under the letters A-E one may consult: S. Gili Gaya, Tesoro lexicográfico (1492-1726), Vol. I:1-4. Madrid: C.S.I.C., Instituto "Antonio de Nebrija," 1947-.

Rostaing, Charles: See under Dauzat, Albert.

Rozwadowski, J. Quaestiones grammaticae et etymologicae. 2 parts. Rozpravy Akad. Wydział Filologičny Krakov., Ser. II, vols. X, XIII; XXV, XXVIII. Krakow, 1897-1900.

Sadnik, Linda, & Rudolf Aizetmüller. Vergleichendes Wörterbuch der slawischen Sprachen. Fasc. 1-2. Wiesbaden: 1963-64.

Sainéan, Lazare. L'argot ancien (1455-1850), ses éléments constitutifs, ses rapports avec les langues secrètes . . . . Paris: H. Champion, 1907.

———. Autour des sources indigènes. Études d'étymologie française et romane. Bibl. dell' "Archivum Romanicum", II:20. Firenze: Leo S. Olschki, 1935.

———. La création métaphorique en français et en roman: Images tirées du monde des animaux domestiques. Suppl. I and X to ZRPh. Halle: M. Niemeyer, 1905-07.

BIBLIOGRAPHY

_____. *Influenţa orientală asupra limbeĭ şi cultureĭ romăne*. 2 vols. Bucureşti: Editura libărieĭ Socecŭ (I), Editura tip. Gutenberg, J. Gŏbl (II), 1900.

_____. *Le langage parisien au XIXᵉ siècle*. Facteurs sociaux, contingents linguistiques, faits sémantiques, influences littéraires. Paris: E. de Boccard, 1920.

_____. *La langue de Rabelais*, 2 vols., II: *Langue et vocabulaire*. Paris: E. de Boccard, 1923.

_____. *Les sources de l'argot ancien*. 2 vols. Paris: H. & É. Champion, 1912.

_____. *Les sources indigènes de l'étymologie française*. 3 vols. Paris: E. de Boccard, 1925-30.

Sánchez, Tomás Antonio (†1802). *Vocabulario de voces anticuadas, para facilitar la lectura de los autores españoles anteriores al siglo XV*. Paris: Baudry, 1842. [Based on glossaries appended to the author's *Colección de poesías castellanas . . .*, 4 vols., Madrid: A. de Sancha, 1779-90.]

Sanchis Guarner, M. See under Alcover, Antoni M.

Scheler, Auguste. *Dictionnaire d'étymologie française d'après les résultats de la science moderne*. Bruxelles: A. Schnée, 1862. Rev. 2d ed. ("entièrement refondue et considérablement augmentée"), Bruxelles: C. Muquardt, & Paris: Maisonneuve & Comp., 1873. 3d ed. ("revue et augmentée"), Bruxelles: T. Falk, 1888.

_____. *Étude lexicologique sur les poésies de Gillon le Muisit*. Préface, glossaire, corrections. Académie Royale, Mémoires, XXXVII. Bruxelles, 1886.

_____. *La geste de Liège par Jehan Des Preis, dit d'Outremeuse*. Académie Royale, Mémoires, XLIV:3. Bruxelles, 1882.

_____. (= "Louis de Landes") *Glossaire érotique de la langue française. . . .* Bruxelles: Chez tous les libraires, 1861.

_____. *Mémoire sur la conjugaison française considérée sous le rapport étymologique*. Académie Royale: Mémoires couronnés, XIX. Bruxelles, 1845.

Schirmer, Alfred. See under Götze, Friedrich.

Schleicher, August. *Compendium der vergleichenden Grammatik der indogermanischen Sprachen*, Weimar: H. Böhlau, 2 vols. in 1, 1861. Rev. 2d ed., 1866. Rev. 3d ed., 1871.

Scholz, Friedrich. *Slavische Etymologie. Eine Anleitung zur Benutzung etymologischer Wörterbücher*. Slavistische Studienbücher, III. Wiesbaden: Otto Harrassowitz, 1966.

Schrader, Otto. "Etymologisch-kulturhistorisches." In: *Philologische Studien: Festgabe für Eduard Sievers*. Halle, 1896.

_____. *Sprachvergleichung und Urgeschichte. Linguistisch-historische Beiträge zur Erforschung des indogermanischen Altertums*. Jena: H. Costenoble, 1883. Rev. 2d ed., 1890. Rev. 3d ed., 2 vols., 1906-7.

Schröer, Arnold M. M. (†1935). *Englisches Handwörterbuch in genetischer Darstellung auf Grund der Etymologien und Bedeutungsentwicklungen . . .*, ed. P. L. Jaeger. 3 vols. Heidelberg: C. Winter, 1937-70.

Schuchardt, Hugo. *Romanische Etymologien*, I-II, in: Akad. Wien, Sitz.-ber., CXXXVIII:1 (1897), and CXLI:3 (1899).

———. *Die romanischen Lehnwörter im Berberischen*. Akad. Wien, Sitz.-ber., CLXXXVIII:4 (1918).

Seebold, Elmar. *Vergleichendes und etymologisches Wörterbuch der germanischen starken Verben*. Janua Linguarum, Series Practica, LXXXV. The Hague & Paris: Mouton, 1970.

Serjeantson, Mary S. *A History of Foreign Words in English*. London: Kegan Paul, Trench, Trubner, & Co., 1935.

Serruys, Paul L.-M. See under Hsüan, Chang.

Siegling, Wilhelm, & Emil Sieg, eds. *Tocharische Sprachreste, Sprache B: Text, Übersetzung und Glossar*. 2 vols. Göttingen: Vandenhoeck & Ruprecht, 1949-53.

Sigart, J. *Glossaire étymologique montois, ou Dictionnaire du wallon de Mons, et de la plus grande partie du Hainaut. (Supplément au Glossaire montois)*. Bruxelles & Leipzig, 1866-68. 2d ed., Bruxelles: F. Claassen, 1870.

Skeat, Walter W. *A Concise Etymological Dictionary of the English Language*. Oxford: Clarendon Press, 1882. Revised eds., 1901, 1911. Repr., 1958, 1961.

———. *An Etymological Dictionary of the English Language*. Oxford: Clarendon Press, [1879-] 1882 (Preface dated 1881). 2d ed., 1883. 3d ed., 1897. New, rev. ed., 1909. Later printings, 1953, 1963.

———. *A List of English Words, the Etymology of which is Illustrated by Comparison with Icelandic*. . . . Oxford: Clarendon Press, 1876.

———. *Mœso-Gothic Glossary; with an Introduction, an Outline of Mœso-Gothic Grammar, and a List of Anglo-Saxon, Old and Modern English Words Etymologically Connected with Mœso-Gothic*. London: Philological Society, 1868.

Skok, Petar. *Dictionnaire étymologique de la langue croate ou serbe*, ed. Mirko Deanović & Liudevit Jonke, with V. Putanec. 2 vols. Zagreb: Académie Yougoslave des Sciences et des Beaux Arts, 1972.

Sławski, Franciszek. *Słownik etymologiczny języka polskiega*. 5 vols. in 4 (A-Juz). Kraków: Nakł. Tow. Miłośników Języka Polskiego, 1952-56.

Solmsen, Felix. *Beiträge zur griechischen Wortforschung*, I. Straβburg: K. J. Trübner, 1909.

Spiegelberg, Wilhelm. *Koptische Etymologien*. Akad. Heidelberg, Sitz.-ber., 1920, No. 27.

———. *Koptisches Handwörterbuch*. Heidelberg: C. Winter, 1921. [An attempt to bring Amadeus Peyron's *Lexicon Linguae Copticae* (Torino, 1835) up to date.]

Spitzer, Leo. *Katalanische Etymologien*. Hamburg: O. Meiβner, 1918 = Suppl. VI to *Jahrbuch der hamburgischen wissenschaftlichen Anstalten*, XXXV (1917).

———. *Lexikalisches aus dem Katalanischen und den übrigen iberoromanischen Sprachen*. Bibl. dell' "Archivum Romanicum," II:1. Genève: Leo S. Olschki, 1921.

———. "A New Spanish Etymological Dictionary" [Corominas, *DCE*], *Modern Language Notes*, LXXI (1956), 271-83, 373-86; LXXII (1957), 579-91; LXXIV (1959), 127-49.

———. Rev. of Américo Castro, *Glosarios latino-españoles de la Edad Media* (1936) in: *Modern Language Notes*, LIII (1938), 122-46.

BIBLIOGRAPHY

Steiger, Arnald. *Contribución a la fonética del hispano-árabe y de los arabismos en el ibero-románico y el siciliano.* Suppl. XVII to the *RFE.* Madrid, 1932.

———. *Contribución al estudio del vocabulario del "Corbacho."* Madrid, 1923. Repr. from *Boletín de la R. Academia Española,* IX (1922), 503-25; X (1923), 26-54; XI (1924), 158-88, 275-93.

Stokes, Whitney. *Urkeltischer Sprachschatz.* Göttingen: Vandenhoeck & Ruprecht, 1894 = A. Fick, *Vergleichendes Wörterbuch* . . ., 4th ed., Part II.

———, and John Strachan, eds. *Thesaurus Palaeohibernicus; a Collection of Old Irish Glosses, Scholia, Prose, and Verse.* 2 vols. Cambridge: University Press, 1901-3. *Supplement:* Halle: M. Niemeyer, 1910.

Stratmann, Francis Henry. *A Middle English Dictionary Containing Words Used by English Writers from the Twelfth to the Fifteenth Century.* New ed., rev. by Henry Bradley. Oxford: Clarendon Press, 1891; repr. 1963. [Goes back to the author's *Dictionary of the Old English Language* . . ., 2d ed., London, 1873.]

Sturtevant, Edgar H. *Hittite Glossary; Words of Known or Conjectured Meaning, with Sumerian Ideograms and Accadian Words Common in Hittite Texts.* "Language" Monograph, IX. Baltimore, 1931. Rev. 2d ed., 1936. Supplement, 1939.

Suárez, Jorge A. "Indigenismos e hispanismos, vistos desde la Argentina" [composite review article], *RPh,* XX (1966-67), 68-90.

———. "Problemas de lexicografía hispano-india" [review article on E. Erize, *Diccionario comentado mapuche-español* (1960), *RPh,* XVII (1963-64), 155-69.]

Šanskij, Nikolaj M. *Ètimologičeskij slovar' russkogo jazyka,* I:1-2. Moskva: Izdatel'stvo Moskovskogo Universiteta, 1963-65.

———. *Frazeologija sovremennogo russkogo jazyka.* Moskva: Vysšaja Škola, 1963. Rev. 2d ed., 1969.

———. *Leksikologija sovremennogo russkogo jazyka.* Moskva: Prosveščenie, 1964. Rev. 2d ed., 1972.

———. *Očerki po russkomu slovoobrazovaniju.* Moskva: Izd. Moskovskogo Universiteta, 1968.

———. *V mire slov.* Moskva: Prosveščenie, 1971.

———, Valerij V. Ivanov, & Tamara V. Šanskaja. *Kratkij ètimologičeskij slovar' russkogo jazyka.* Moskva: Gosudarstvenno-Pedagogičeskoe Izdatel'stvo, 1961. Rev. 2d ed. (Preface by S. G. Barxudarov), Moskva: Prosveščenie, 1971.

Tagliavini, Carlo, ed. *Il "Lexicon Marsilianum"; dizionario latino-rumeno-ungherese del secolo XVII.* Studio filologico e testo. Academia Română: Études et recherches, V. Bucureşti: Cultura Naţională, 1930.

Tamm, Fredrik (†1905). *Etymologisk svensk ordbok.* 2 vols. (A-Karsk). Preface by A. Noreen. Uppsala: Akademiska Boktryckeriet E. Berling, 1890-1905.

Tappolet, Ernst. *Die romanischen Verwandtschaftsnamen, mit besonderer Berücksichtigung der französischen und italienischen Mundarten. Ein Beitrag zur vergleichenden Lexikologie.* Straßburg: K. J. Trübner, 1895.

Thomas, Antoine. *Mélanges d'étymologie française.* Université de Paris: Bibliothèque de la Faculté des Lettres, XIV. Paris: F. Alcan, 1902. 2d ed. ("revue et augmentée"), Collection linguistique (Soc. de Ling. de Paris),

XXII. Paris: H. Champion, 1927. [A long-planned 2d series failed to materialize.] See also under Darmesteter, Arsène, et al.

Thurneysen, Rudolf. *Die Etymologie; eine akademische Rede.* Freiburg im Breisgau: Speyer & Kärner, 1905.

———. *Keltoromanisches. Die keltischen Etymologien im "Etymologischen Wörterbuch der romanischen Sprachen"* [3d ed. and reprints] *von F. Diez.* Halle: M. Niemeyer, 1884.

Tietze, Andreas: See under Kahane, Henry & Renée.

Tiktin, Hariton. *Dicţionar român-german. Rumänisch-deutsches Wörterbuch.* 3 vols. Bucureşti: Staatsdruckerei, 1903-28.

Tobler, Adolf (†1910), & Erhard Lommatzsch. *Altfranzösisches Wörterbuch.* 10 vols. (*A-Ru*). Berlin: Weidemann, 1925-74 (continued).

Torp, Alf (†1916). *Nynorsk etymologisk ordbok,* ed. M. Haegstad and H. Falk, Kristiania: H. Aschehoug & Co. (W. Nygaard), 1915-19 (issued in parts). See also under Falk, Hjalmar.

Trautmann, Reinhold. *Die altpreußischen Sprachdenkmäler; Einleitung, Texte, Grammatik, Wörterbuch.* Göttingen: Vandenhoeck & Ruprecht, 1910.

———. *Baltisch-slawisches Wörterbuch.* Göttinger Sammlung indogermanischer Grammatiken und Wörterbücher. Göttingen: Vandenhoeck & Ruprecht, 1923.

Trubačev, O. N. See under Vasmer, Max.

Tucker, T[homas] G[eorge]. *A Concise Etymological Dictionary of Latin.* Halle: M. Niemeyer, 1931.

Turner, Lorenzo D. *Africanisms in the Gullah Dialect* [coastal region of South Carolina and Georgia]. Chicago: University of Chicago Press, 1949.

Turner, Ralph L. *A Comparative Dictionary of the Indo-Aryan Languages.* 2 vols. London & New York: Oxford University Press, 1962-66. *Indexes,* comp. Dorothy Rivers Turner. Oxford University Press, 1969.

———. *A Comparative and Etymological Dictionary of the Nepali Language.* London: K. Paul, Trench, Trubner, and Co., 1931. Repr. (with corrections, and "with indexes of all words quoted from other I.-E. languages," comp. Dorothy Rivers Turner), Routledge & K. Paul, 1965.

Uhlenbeck, C. C. *Kurzgefaßtes etymologisches Wörterbuch der altindischen Sprache.* Amsterdam: J. Müller, 1898-99; 2d ed. (1900).

———. *Kurzgefaßtes etymologisches Wörterbuch der gotischen Sprache.* Amsterdam: J. Müller, 1896. Rev. 2d ed., 1900.

——— *Die lexikalische Urverwandtschaft des Baltoslawischen und Germanischen.* Leiden: Blankenberg, 1890. Cf. his Leyden diss. (1888): *De verwantschapsbetrekkingen tusschen de germaansche en baltoslavische talen.*

———. *De oudere lagen van den baskischen woordenschat.* Akad. van Wet., Letterkunde, Verh., N.R., V:7 Amsterdam: Noord-Hollandsche Uitgevers Maatschappij, 1942.

———, with R. H. van Gulik. *An English-Blackfoot Vocabulary, Based on Material from the Southern Peigans.* Akad. van Wet., Letterkunde, Verh., N.R., XXIX:4. Amsterdam, 1930.

——— ———. *A Blackfoot-English Vocabulary.* Ibid., XXXIII:2. Amsterdam: Noord-Hollandsche Uitgevers-Maatschappij, 1934.

Vasmer, Max. *Ètimologičeskij slovar' russkogo jazyka*. 3 vols. Tr. (and elab.) O. N. Trubačëv; ed. B. A. Larin. Moskva: Progress, 1964-71.

———. *Russisches etymologisches Wörterbuch*. 3 vols. Indogermanische Bibliothek, II: Wörterbücher. Heidelberg: C. Winter, 1953-58. Rev. (and elab.) R. Jakobson, *Word*, VII (1951), 187-91; VIII (1952), 387-94; XI (1955), 611-17.

———, dir. *Wörterbuch der russischen Gewässernamen*, comp. A. Kernd'l, Rosemarie Richhardt, W. Eisold. Veröffentlichungen des Slawischen Seminars, Freie Universität Berlin, XXII (1961-).

———, Ingrid Coper, Herbert Bräuer, et al. *Russisches geographisches Namenbuch*. Akademie der Wissenschaften und der Literatur, Mainz. Wiesbaden: O. Harrassowitz, 1964-.

Vendryes, Joseph. *Lexique étymologique de l'irlandais ancien*. 2 vols. (*A, M-P*). Dublin: Institute for Advanced Studies, & Paris: Centre National de la Recherche Scientifique, 1959-61.

Vercoullie, Jozef. *Beknopt etymologisch woordenboek der Nederlandsche taal*. Gent: J. Vuylsteke, 1890. Rev. 2d ed. ("verbeterde en zeer vermeerterde uitgave"), 1898. 3d ed., 's-Gravenhage: M. Nijhoff, Gent: Van Rysselberghe & Rombaut, 1925. Cf. C. C. Uhlenbeck's 12-page rev. ("Aant eekeningen . . .") in: *Taal en Letteren*, 1899.

———. *Dictionnaire français-néerlandais et néerlandais-français*. "Nouv. éd. corrigée et augmentée." Sottagem: "De Beiaard," 1948.

Verrier, A. J., & R. Onillon. *Glossaire étymologique et historique des patois et des parlers de l'Anjou, comprenant . . . des dialogues, contes, récits. . . .* 2 vols., folding map. Angers: Germain & G. Grassin, 1908.

Vieira, Frei Domingos. *Grande dicionário português, ou, Tesouro da língua portuguesa*. 5 vols. Porto: E. Chardron & B. H. de Moraes, 1871-74. (Vol. I contains F. A. Coelho's treatise, *Sobre a língua portuguesa;* Vol. II a reader: *Crestomatia histórica da língua portuguesa*.)

von den Steinen, Dietrich. See under Emeneau, Murray B.

Voretzsch, Carl (later Karl). *Einführung in das Studium der altfranzösischen Sprache zum Selbstunterricht. . . .* Sammlung kurzer Lehrbücher . . ., I. Halle: Niemeyer, 1901. 2d ed., 1903. Rev. 3d ed., 1907. 4th ed., 1911. 5th ed., 1918. 6th ed., 1932. 7th ed., rev. by G. Rohlfs, 1951. 8th ed., 1955.

Vries, Jan de. *Altnordisches etymologisches Wörterbuch*. Issued in parts. Leiden: E. J. Brill, 19[57-]61. Rev. 2d ed., 1962.

Wagner, Max Leopold. *Dizionario etimologico sardo*. 3 vols., issued in 23 parts. Heidelberg: C. Winter, 1957-64. (Vol. III: *Indici* . . ., comp. Raffaele G. Urciolo.)

Walde, Alois. *Lateinisches etymologisches Wörterbuch*. Sammlung indogermanischer Lehrbücher, dir. H. Hirt & W. Streitberg, II:1. Issued in 10 parts. Heidelberg: C. Winter, 19[05]-06. Rev. 2d ed., 1910. For the 3d ed. (1938-54), see under Hofmann, J. B.

———, and Julius Pokorny. *Vergleichendes Wörterbuch der indogermanischen Sprachen*. 3 vols. Berlin & Leipzig: W. de Gruyter & Co., 1927-32. Vol. III, the *Registerband*, was compiled by Konstantin Reichardt.

Walshe, M[aurice] O'C[onnell]. *A Concise German Etymological Dictionary*.

London: Routledge & K. Paul, 1951[-52]. (With a Supplement on the Etymology of Some Middle High German Words Extinct in Modern German, by Marianne Winder.)

Wartburg, Walther von. *Französisches etymologisches Wörterbuch. Eine Darstellung des galloromanischen Wortschatzes.* Issued in parts. Vols. I-X, XIV, XVI (*Germanische Elemente*). Vol. I, Bonn & Leipzig: F. Klopp, 19[22]-28. Later volumes, Basel: Helbing & Lichtenhahn. Companion volumes: (a) *Ortsnamenregister, Literaturverzeichnis, Übersichtskarte,* 2d ed., Tübingen: J. C. B. Mohr (Paul Siebeck), 1950; (b) (α) *Bibliographie des dictionnaires patois,* comp. W. von W., Publ. rom. et frç. (dir. M. Roques), VIII; Paris: E. Droz, 1934; (β) *Supplément (1934-55),* comp. H.-E. Keller & J. Renson, Publ. rom. et frç., LII; Paris: E. Droz, 1955; (γ) *Bibliographie des dictionnaires patois galloromans (1550-1967),* Publ. rom. et frç., CIII, comp. W. von W., H.-E. Keller, & Robert Geuljans.

Wasserzieher, Ernst (†1927). *Woher? Ableitendes Wörterbuch der deutschen Sprache.* Rev. 5th ed., Berlin: F. Dümmler, 1922. 12th ed., rev. Paul Herthum, Bonn & Berlin: F. Dümmler, 1950. 15th ed., rev. Werner Betz, Bonn: F. Dümmler, 1962. 16th ed., 1963. 17th ed., 1966.

Weekley, Ernest (†1954). *A Concise Etymological Dictionary of Modern English.* Rev. ed., New York: E. P. Dutton, 1952.

――――. *An Etymological Dictionary of Modern English.* London: John Murray, 1912. Repr., 2 vols., New York: Dover Publications, 1967.

――――. *Etymologies, Chiefly Anglo-French.* Read at the Meeting of the Philological Society on Feb. 4, 1910.

――――. *Jack and Jill; a Study in Our Christian Names.* New York: E. P. Dutton, 1940.

Wessén, Elias. *Våra ord, deras uttal och ursprung; kortfattad etymologisk ordbok.* Rev. ed., Stockholm: Svenska bokförlaget, 1961.

Wijk, N. van. See under Franck, Johannes.

Williams, Edwin B. *Spanish & English Dictionary; Diccionario inglés & español.* New York: Henry Holt & Cie., 1955.

Windekens, Albert J. van. *Lexique étymologique des dialectes tokhariens.* Bibliothèque du *Muséon,* XI. Louvain: Bureaux du *Muséon,* 1941.

Windisch, Ernst. See under Curtius, Georg.

Winkel, Jan te. See under Franck, Johannes.

Wölfflin, Eduard von, ed. *Archiv für lateinische Lexikographie und Grammatik, mit Einschluß des älteren Mittellateins.* 15 vols. Leipzig: 1884-1908. Sponsored by the Bavarian Academy of Sciences.

Wüst, Walther. *Vergleichendes und etymologisches Wörterbuch des Alt-Indoiranischen (Altindischen).* Indogermanische Bibliothek, I:4. Heidelberg: C. Winter, 19[33]-35.

Zambaldi, Francesco. *Vocabolario etimologico italiano.* Castello, 1899. Rev. 2d ed. ("con appendice dei nomi di persona"), 1913.

Zauner, Adolf. *Die romanischen Namen der Körperteile.* Erlangen, 1902. (Repr. from *Romanische Forschungen,* XIV:1:339-530 [1903]).

Zeitschrift für deutsche Wortforschung = Vols. I-XIX of *Zeitschrift für deutsche Sprache,* ed. Friedrich Kluge. Straßburg, 1900-14.

Zeuss, [J.] Kaspar (†1856). "Index Vocabulorum" to *Grammatica Celtica, e*

BIBLIOGRAPHY

monumentis vetustis tam Hibernicae linguae quam Britannicae. .... 2 vols.
Leipzig: Weidmann, 1853. 2d ed., rev. by Hermann Ebel, Berlin: Weidmann,
1871. (A Supplement to the Glossary is attached to Edmund Hogan's ed.
of *Cath Ruis na Ríg,* Dublin: Royal Irish Academy – Todd Lecture Series,
1892).

Zgusta, Ladislav, et al. *Manual of Lexicography.* Praha: Academia (Czechoslovak
Academy of Sciences), 1971.

INDEX

This master list contains references to names of languages and of scholars cited, as well as to concepts, key-terms, themes, styles, and subdisciplines of linguistic science. Neither titles of books nor lexical illustrations have been included.

INDEX

character of a dictionary, 7
characteristic descendant, 68
charter (as evidence), 23
Chinese, 19
chrestomathy and dictionary, 72
chronological dictionary, 24
chronological information, 24
Chukchic, 33
Cihac, A. de, 18, 32, 77
Cioranescu, A., 18
classificatory canons, 2
Clédat, L., 21, 24, 81
codification of knowledge, 82, 84
coding of dictionaries, 8, 81
Coelho, F. A., 92
cognate, 5, 45, 56, 57, 66, 68, 69
Cohen, M., 38
Cohn, G., 60
collaborative project, 16, 17
collection of short notes, 72
collective numeral, 77
colloquial discourse, 53, 75
color adjectives, 11, 38
commercial interests, 7, 9, 21, 25, 27, 76
"Common Aryan," 3
common denominator (in semantics), 12
commonness of occurrence, 7, 41
compactness, 35, 64
comparative dictionary, 2, 3, 13, 26, 27, 28, 33, 41, 51, 68, 83
comparative grammar, 58, 68
competing forms, 35, 43
complementarity of dictionaries, mutual, 61
composite entry, 35
composite etymological dictionary, 78
compound, 4, 23, 26, 29, 36, 43, 47, 57, 63, 71
compression of documentation and analysis, 41
concentration (tightening), 37
concise dictionary, 41, 58
concordance, 7, 9, 74
conflicting hypotheses, 22
congener, 20, 21
conjecture, 43

connection (lexical), 80
connotation, 23
consolidation of entries, 36, 37
contact between lexical families, 65
contamination (= blend), 64
contrastive grammar, 1
controversial etymology, 39, 55
Coptic, ix
Corblet, J., 10
Cornish, 57
Corominas, J., 5, 6, 11, 16, 41, 44, 66, 74, 77, 78, 79, 93, 94
corpus (of data, of hypotheses), 3, 11, 59
corrections, 66
counterparts in lexicography, 18
counterview, 68
Covarrubias (H)orozco, S. de, 4, 26, 42, 44, 50
critical comment, 5, 6, 11
cross-linguistic dictionary, 7
cross-reference, 4, 25, 36, 49, 63
crossing, 64
Cuervo, R. J., 10, 25
cultural history (or context), 38, 44, 47, 54, 58, 63
cultural index, 38
culturally-associated language, 4
curiosity about language, 78, 79
Curtius, G., 88
cyclic view of scholarship, 33
Cymric, 57
Cyrillic script, 19, 46

Daco-Romance, 45
Dalmatian, 57
Danish, 17, 18, 57, 61, 68, 70
Darmesteter, A., 10, 16, 81, 92
data vs. analysis, 5
dating (absolute, relative), 24, 51, 57
"daughter language," 2, 25, 27, 50
Dauzat, A., 6, 14, 16, 21, 24, 52, 57, 89
dead language, 7, 79
débris or flotsam (lexical), 36
decorum, 81
definitive introduction, 24
Delbrück, B., 12, 77

133

INDEX

Scythian, 69
secondary contact, 62
secondary homonyms, 62
secondary (tertiary) shift, 6
selection, selectivity, 8, 40, 61, 87
self-appraisal (self-characterization), 6
semantic common denominator, 85
semantic dictionary, 12, 73
semantic index, 92
semantic nuance, 4, 5, 57, 58
semantic relation, 34, 36, 48, 49, 62, 63, 77
semantic shift, 94
semasiology (= old-style semantics), 69
Semitic, 46
semo-etymology, 9
separate listing (of words, components), 36, 62, 89
sequence of events, 80
Serbian (Serbocroatian), 19, 22
seriousness of research, 79
Serra, G. D., 60
Serruys, P. L.-M., 19
Shetlandic, 58
shorter etymological dictionary, 9
Sicilian, 14, 31
side issue (etymological), 73
sigla, 51
Sigling, W., 29
Sin(g)halese, 59
single language (in comparative perspective), 86
Skeat, W. W., 19, 24, 35, 36, 52, 66, 67, 70, 71, 91, 92
skeletal etymological dictionary, 28
skepticism, dosages and voicing of, 54, 61
Slavic, 2, 12, 15, 22, 23, 26, 29, 31, 40, 41, 46, 61, 66, 69, 87, 93
Proto-Slavic, 40
Slavisms, 76
Slavo-Germanic, 3
social dialect, 23
socioeducational status, 51
sociolinguistics, 51
Sogdian, 69
solution (in etymology), 82
sophistication of analysis, 83

sound correspondence, 64, 72
source (primary, secondary), 55, 75
source language, 2, 29, 30, 31, 39
Spanish, 4, 6, 7, 10, 16, 17, 18, 25, 26, 30, 31, 40, 41, 48, 66, 69, 70, 80, 90
Golden Age Spanish, 74
Old Spanish, 6, 42, 62, 71, 74
spatio-temporal linguistics, vii, 3, 22
specialist's view, 9
speculative etymology, 56
spelling habits, 34, 73
Spiegelberg, W., 8
Spitzer, L., 40, 77, 78
splitting of languages, 27
spontaneous creation (= Urschöpfung), 80
spurious form, 51
standard dictionary, 94
standard (form, word, language), 75, 88
Steiger, A., 31
"steps," number of, 21
straight history, 87, 89
"strains" or "streaks" (lexical), 4, 7, 77
strata (= layers) of the lexicon, 52
strategy in etymology, 82, 84
Stratmann, F. H., 42
string of monographs, 86
stringency of presentation, 43
string of etymological notes, 12
structuralism, 4
Sturtevant, E. H., 18
style, stylistics, 5, 7
styling of etymological research, 84
stylistic level, 51
stylistic shift or variation, 53, 94
Suárez, J., 32
subclass of dictionaries, 12
subfamily, 50
subfield of linguistics, 81
subjectivism, 16
"substratal" (base, language), 2, 3, 23, 86, 94
subsumption, levels of, 49
subtitle, 88
suffixation, 70

142

INDEX

variant, 35, 36, 58
Vasmer, M., 3, 17, 19, 61, 65, 66
Vendryes, J., 17, 79
verbal illustration, 11
verb (troublesome), 56
verb of motion, 11
Vercouillie, J., 79
verdict on controversial issue, 9
vernacular reflex, 5
veterinary lexicon, 90
Vietnamese, 14
vignette (lexical), 43
vocabulary, 10, 11, 71, 78
von den Steinen, D., 14
Vor-, Nach-arbeiten, 87
Vordatierung, 25
Voretzsch, C. (or K.), 72

Wagner, M. L., 75, 78
Walde, A., 5, 16, 17, 27, 39, 45, 48,
  56, 59, 61

Wartburg, W. von, 5, 6, 8, 13, 16, 17,
  18, 24, 25, 39, 40, 43, 44, 51, 53,
  58, 60, 61, 64, 69, 74, 79
wave ("vogue") of words, 25
Weekley, E., 24, 66, 91
Whitney, W. D., vii
Williams, E. B., 91
Windisch, E., 88
Wölfflin, E., 75
Wörter und Sachen, 38
word biography, 6, 18
word family, 36
workmanship, 83

Zauner, A., 12, 94
Zend (= Old Bactrian, Avesta), 15, 51,
  92
Zgusta, L., 89, 91
zoonym, 12, 92
Zumthor, P., 17